coding
Games
in PYTHON®

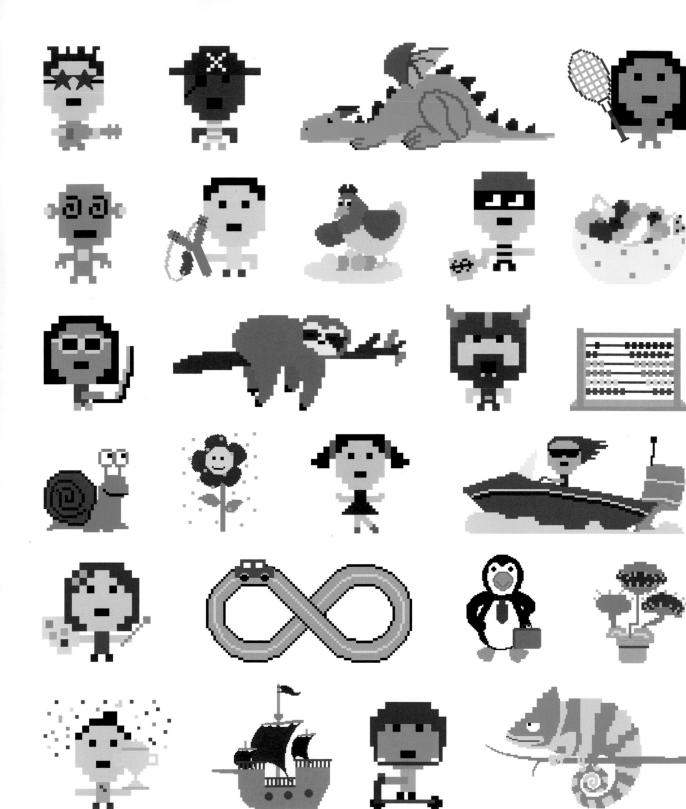

coding
games
in PYTHON®

DK UK

Project editor Ben Ffrancon Davies
Senior art editor Sunita Gahir
Consultant editor Craig Steele
Jacket design development manager Sophia MTT
Jacket editor Claire Gell
Producer, pre-production Gillian Reid
Senior Producer Alex Bell
US editors Jill Hamilton, Kayla Dugger
Managing editor Lisa Gillespie
Managing art editor Owen Peyton Jones
Publisher Andrew Macintyre
Associate publishing director Liz Wheeler
Art director Karen Self
Design director Phil Ormerod
Publishing director Jonathan Metcalf

DK INDIA

Senior editor Bharti Bedi
Project art editor Sanjay Chauhan
Editor Tina Jindal
Assistant art editors Rabia Ahmad,
Simar Dhamija, Sonakshi Singh
Jacket designer Juhi Sheth
Jackets editorial coordinator Priyanka Sharma
Managing jackets editor Saloni Singh
DTP designer Sachin Gupta
Senior DTP designer Harish Aggarwal
Senior managing editor Rohan Sinha
Managing art editor Sudakshina Basu
Pre-production manager Balwant Singh

First American Edition, 2018
Published in the United States by DK Publishing
345 Hudson Street, New York, New York 10014

A catalog record for this book
is available from the Library of Congress.
ISBN: 978-1-4654-7361-5

Printed in China

A WORLD OF IDEAS:
SEE ALL THERE IS TO KNOW

www.dk.com

CAROL VORDERMAN MBE is one of Britain's best-loved TV presenters and is renowned for her mathematical skills. She has hosted numerous TV shows on science and technology, from *Tomorrow's World* to *How 2*, and was co-host of Channel 4's *Countdown* for 26 years. A Cambridge University engineering graduate, she has a passion for communicating science and technology and is particularly interested in coding.

CRAIG STEELE is a specialist in computing science education who helps people develop digital skills in a fun and creative environment. He is a founder of CoderDojo in Scotland, which runs free coding clubs for young people. Craig has run digital workshops with the Raspberry Pi Foundation, Glasgow Science Centre, Glasgow School of Art, BAFTA, and the BBC micro:bit project. Craig's first computer was a ZX Spectrum.

DR. CLAIRE QUIGLEY studied computing science at Glasgow University, where she obtained BSc and PhD degrees. She has worked in the Computer Laboratory at Cambridge University and Glasgow Science Centre, and is currently working on a project to develop a music and technology resource for primary schools in Edinburgh. She is a mentor at CoderDojo Scotland.

DANIEL McCAFFERTY holds a degree in computer science from the University of Strathclyde. He has worked as a software engineer for companies big and small in industries from banking to broadcasting. Daniel lives in Glasgow with his wife and two children, and when not teaching young people to code, he enjoys bicycling and spending time with his family.

DR. MARTIN GOODFELLOW is a teaching associate in the Computer and Information Sciences department at the University of Strathclyde. He has also developed educational computer science content and workshops for other organizations in the UK and China, including CoderDojo Scotland, Glasgow Life, Codemao, and the BBC. He is currently the Scottish Ambassador for National Coding Week.

Contents

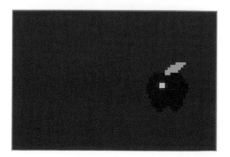

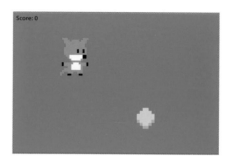

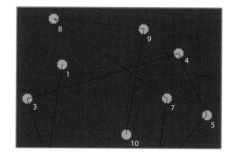

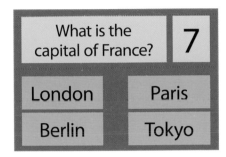

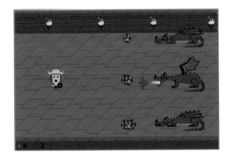

Foreword

Computer programmers are the unsung heroes of the modern world. From smartphones to laptops, traffic systems to bank cards, their hard work touches almost every aspect of our lives. Behind each technological advance is a team of creative coders.

Over the past 30 years, computer games have become one of the most exciting and popular areas of the entertainment industry to work in. Becoming a game programmer takes creative flair to help create the story, graphics, music, and characters you need for your games, and the technical know-how to bring them to life. Who knows? This book may be the very first step on your journey from gamer to game maker.

Learning to code isn't just for people who want to be professional programmers, though. Coding skills are useful in lots of different jobs that may seem to have nothing to do with computers at first. Programming expertise is essential to subject areas as diverse as science, business, art, and music.

This book uses a programming language called Python®, a fairly simple text-based language, and is perfect for beginners, or as a step up from Scratch™. However, unlike Scratch, it was not created especially to teach coding. Python is as popular with budding coders as it is with professionals, and is one of the most widely used professional programming languages in the world. It pops up in banking, medicine, animation, and even space exploration.

The best way to learn any new language is to get immersed in it, and programming languages are no different. Building your own computer games is a fun way to combine theory and practice. If you're a brand-new coder, start off with the basics at the beginning of this book before moving on to the more complex games as the book progresses. By following the step-by-step guides, you'll find out how professional coders think when they're building a computer game. Follow those steps carefully and you'll have your own games up and running in no time. Then, if you really want to push yourself, you can try tweaking the code to make your games unique.

Everybody, whether a beginner or a pro, makes mistakes. Nothing frustrates a coder more than the bugs that manage to creep into their programs. If something goes wrong in one of your games, go back over your code and check it all carefully. There are hints and tips throughout the book that will help you do this. Most importantly, don't get disheartened—finding and fixing errors in your code is all part of being a programmer. The more practice you get, the fewer bugs your code will contain, and the quicker you'll catch the little ones that still appear.

Most importantly, have fun! Once you've completed the games, you can show them off to your friends and family—they'll be amazed by what you've managed to make. This book is packed with games to suit every audience, and we hope you enjoy building and playing them as much as we enjoyed creating them for you.

Have fun coding!

Getting started

What is Python?

Computers need step-by-step instructions to perform different tasks. A set of instructions, or code, can be written in different programming languages. Python is one of the most popular programming languages.

Python is great!
I can take
it anywhere.

Why Python?

Python is a powerful programming language that you can use to code simple programs quickly. It's not too hard to learn and it's great for building apps and games. Here are some of the reasons why Python is such a great tool for programmers.

△ **Portable**
The same Python code will work on PCs, Macs, Linux machines, and Raspberry Pi computers. The programs act in a similar way on each platform, so games created with Python can be played on lots of machines all around the world.

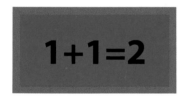

$$1+1=2$$

△ **Easy to understand**
Unlike some other programming languages, Python doesn't use complicated symbols. You type the code using a mixture of English words, characters, and numbers, so it's easy to read and write—just like a book.

◁ **Diverse applications**
Python is used to build systems and tools for lots of interesting tasks in different industries, such as banking, healthcare, the space industry, education, and many others.

Better get started!

△ **Packed with tools**
Python comes with everything you need to start coding right away, so programmers say it comes with "batteries included." It contains lots of prewritten code, called the Standard Library, that you can use in your programs.

△ **Lots of help**
Python's website is packed with support materials to help you learn how to use it. It has a guide to getting started, several pieces of sample code, and a reference section to help you understand the code.

From Scratch to Python

Scratch is a visual language, whereas Python is text based. If you've used Scratch, you will recognize some of the features and ideas in Python. The two languages might look different, but lots of the elements that are used in Scratch are also used in Python.

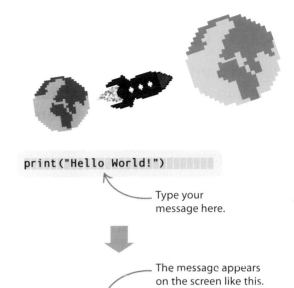

```
print("Hello World!")
```

Type your message here.

The message appears on the screen like this.

```
Hello World!
```

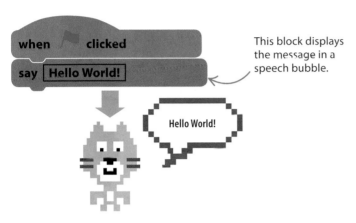

This block displays the message in a speech bubble.

△ **Print in Scratch**
In Scratch, the "say" block is used to display a message on the screen.

△ **Print in Python**
In Python, the "print" command displays a message on the screen.

This command is executed if the condition after **if** is True.

This message is displayed if the answer is True.

This is the end of the "if-then-else" block.

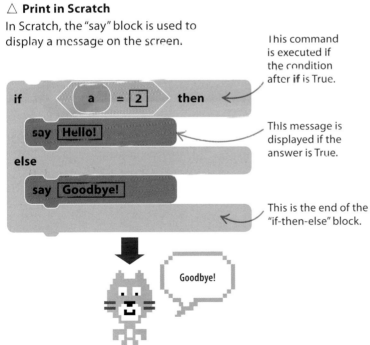

```
if a == 2:
    print("Hello!")
else:
    print("Goodbye!")
```

This message is displayed if the answer is False.

This command is executed if the condition after **if** is False.

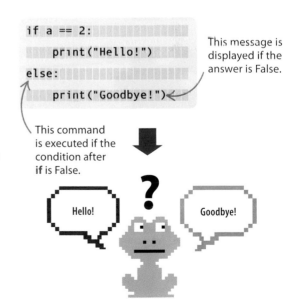

△ **Set a condition with Scratch**
The "if-then-else" block lets you choose which part of the script to run depending on whether the condition is True or False.

△ **Set a condition with Python**
In Python, "if-then-else" commands work exactly the same way, but they don't use the word "then."

Gaming in Python

Video games are computer programs that contain a bunch of instructions. Python can be used to build lots of different types of games. With Python, there's something for every gamer!

Types of games

There are lots of different categories, or genres, of computer games. These range from simple one-button games to more complex strategy ones. Which genre would you like to create first?

▷ **One button**

With Python, you can build fun, action-packed games that only need one button to be played. These games are so addictive, you'll want to play them over and over again.

◁ **Puzzles**

Puzzles are a great way to exercise your brain or test someone's general knowledge. They come in all shapes and sizes, from jigsaw puzzles to word and number games.

△ **Platform**

Platform games, such as racing games, create the illusion of speed by making the background scroll past the player's viewpoint. The gameplay generally involves moving around obstacles or jumping over them.

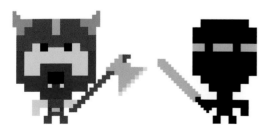

△ **Multiplayer**

Some games you play by yourself, but others let you compete against other players. You can use Python to build multiplayer games and challenge your friends.

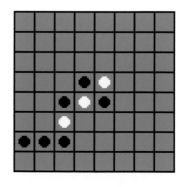

◁ **Strategy**

A strategy game is all about decisions. You need to plan ahead and make the right choices to win.

Python modules

Python has bundles of code called "modules" that help you complete common coding tasks. You can use these modules by importing them into your programs. Here are some Python modules that you might find useful.

▽ Pygame

Pygame is designed for writing games in Python. With this module, you can easily add and control game characters, update scores and timers, use special animations and graphics, and use gamepads and joysticks with your games. It is not a built-in Python module, so it needs to be installed separately.

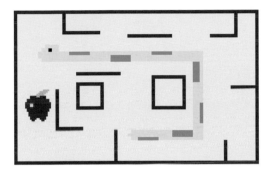

◁ Pygame Zero

Pygame Zero is a great module for beginner game programmers. It's a simplified version of Pygame, which makes it even easier to get started by hiding some of Pygame's more complicated features. It comes with several tools that are useful for beginners, but it's also powerful enough to build some impressive games.

▷ Math

Math is a standard Python module that can be used to perform simple calculations in games. However, you might need to use other modules for trickier calculations.

▷ Random

This module can pick a random number or shuffle a list into a random order. It is great for adding an element of chance to a game. Use it when you want to simulate rolling dice or when choosing a random enemy for the player to face.

◁ Time

This module provides tools to work with time and dates in a program. For example, you might need to calculate how many seconds have passed since a game started.

◁ Tkinter

This tool is used to build simple graphics in games to create Graphical User Interfaces (GUIs, pronounced "goo-eys") that let users interact with, and control, Python programs.

Installing Python

The games in this book use Python 3. It's free, and you can download it from the Python website. Follow the instructions that match your computer. Never install any program unless you have the computer owner's permission.

Installing Python on Windows

First you need to find out if your computer uses the 32-bit or 64-bit version of Windows. Go to the **Start** menu, then **Computer**, **Properties**, and choose **System** if the option appears.

 LINGO

IDLE

When you install Python 3, you will also get another free program called IDLE (short for Integrated Development Environment). Designed for beginners, IDLE includes a basic text editor that allows you to write and edit Python code.

1 **Download Python**
Go to www.python.org and click on **Downloads**. Click on the latest version of Python for Windows. It should start with the number 3. Select **executable installer** from the different installer options that appear.

The version number might not be exactly the same as this one—just make sure it has 3 at the beginning.

- Python 3.6.2 - 2017-05-15
  - Windows x86 executable installer
  - Windows x86-64 executable installer

Use this installer if you have a 32-bit version of Windows.

Use this installer if you have a 64-bit version of Windows.

2 **Install Python**
Open the installer file, then click **Custom Installation**, then **Next** until you get to **Advanced Options**. Leave the checked boxes as they are, but make sure "Install for all users" and "Add Python to environment variables" are also checked. Then click **Install** and **Next** at each prompt.

Click the installer.

3 **Start IDLE**
Once the installation process is complete, open IDLE by searching for it or going to the **Start** menu, choosing **All Apps**, then selecting **IDLE**. A window like the one below should appear.

```
                    Python 3.6.2 Shell
IDLE    File    Edit    Shell    Debug    Window    Help

Python 3.6.2 (v3.6.2:5fd3365926, Aug 15 2017, 00:45:10) [MSC v.1900 32 bit
(Intel)] on win32
Type "copyright", "credits" or "license()" for more information.
>>>
```

Installing Python on a Mac

Before you install Python 3 on a Mac, you need to check which operating system your Mac uses. To do this, click the **Apple** icon in the top left of the screen and choose **About This Mac** from the drop-down menu.

1 Download Python
Go to www.python.org and click on **Downloads**. Click on the version of Python 3 that matches your operating system. The "Python.pkg" file will download to your Mac automatically.

The version number might not be exactly the same as this one—just make sure it has a 3 at the beginning.

- Python 3.6.2 - 2017-08-15
  - Download macOS X 64-bit/32-bit installer

2 Install Python
Double-click the ".pkg" file in the **Downloads** folder to start the installation. Select **Continue** and then **Install** to accept the default settings.

Click the package to run the installer.

3 Start IDLE
Once the installation is complete, check that it was successful by opening the IDLE program. Search for it in Spotlight or select the **Applications** folder, then the **Python** folder, and double-click **IDLE**. A window like this should appear.

Where should I plug this in?

I better get going!

```
                    Python 3.6.2 Shell
IDLE    File    Edit    Shell    Debug    Window    Help
Python 3.6.2 (v3.6.2:5fd3365926, Aug 15 2017, 13:38:16)
[GCC 4.2.1 (Apple Inc. build 5666) (dot 3)] on darwin
Type "copyright", "credits" or "license()" for more information.
>>>
```

Installing Pygame Zero

Now it's time to add some extra tools to help you build great games. In this book, you'll need two additional modules—Pygame and Pygame Zero. These are not included with Python, so you need to install them separately.

EXPERT TIPS

Admin access

Make sure you're signed into your computer as an admin; otherwise, the system won't let you install things properly. Always ask permission before installing new software on someone's computer.

Installing Pygame Zero on Windows

Follow these steps to install the latest versions of Pygame and Pygame Zero on your Windows computer. Your machine needs to be connected to the Internet to complete some of these steps.

1 Open the Command Prompt
Click **Start**. Scroll down and open the **Windows System** folder. Click **Command Prompt**. If you can't find it, try searching for it. You'll need to type in some commands and press **Enter** to run each one. Make sure you spell everything correctly and put spaces in the right places or it won't work.

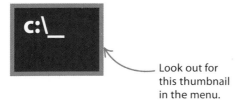

Look out for this thumbnail in the menu.

2 Install a package manager
A package manager called "pip" should come with Python when you install it. It's a tool that makes it easier to install Pygame Zero and other Python modules. Type this command into the Command Prompt and press **Enter**—it will check if pip is on your computer and install it if it is not.

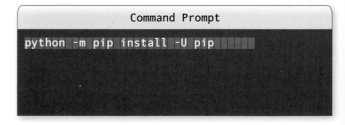

Command Prompt

python -m pip install -U pip

3 Install Pygame
Once the package manager is installed, type the following command and press **Enter**. This uses pip to install Pygame.

`pip install pygame`

4 Install Pygame Zero
Finally, type this command. When you press **Enter**, this will install Pygame Zero, also known as pgzero for short.

`pip install pgzero`

Installing Pygame Zero on a Mac

Follow these steps to install the latest versions of Pygame and Pygame Zero on your Mac. Your machine needs to be connected to the Internet to complete some of these steps.

 1 Open Terminal

You'll need to use the Terminal app to install the modules. You can find it in your **Applications** folder, or you can search for it with Spotlight. Follow the steps below, making sure all the spellings are correct and the spaces are in the right place.

 2 Install a package manager

Homebrew is a package manager tool that makes it easier to install Pygame Zero and other Python modules. Type in the command at right and press **Enter** to install Homebrew. It might ask you to enter your password again, and It will take a short while to install, so don't panic if nothing happens right away.

 3 Check that Python 3 is installed

Homebrew will check if Python 3 is already installed on your Mac and will install it if it's not there. Even though you've already installed Python, it's worth checking just to be sure.

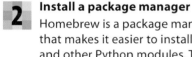 **4 Install other tools**

Type in this command next and press **Enter**. It uses Homebrew to install some tools that will be needed by Pygame Zero.

 5 Install Pygame

Now it's time to install Pygame. Type in this command and press **Enter**.

 6 Install Pygame Zero

Finally, this last command will install Pygame Zero.

This is what the Terminal app thumbnail looks like.

Type this line carefully In the Terminal window and check for any spelling errors and extra spaces.

```
🏠 Rabiahma – bash – 80x24

Last login: Thu Sep 14 11:22:51 on ttys000
LC-0926:~ rzvz ruby -e "$(curl -fsSL https://raw.git
hubusercontent.com/Homebrew/install/master/install)"
```

This should fit on one line when you type it in.

```
brew install python3
```

Don't put a space before **3**.

```
brew install sdl sdl_mixer sdl_sound sdl_ttf
```

```
pip3 install pygame
```

```
pip3 install pgzero
```

INSTALLING

Using IDLE

In IDLE, you can work in two different windows. The editor window can be used to write and save programs, while the shell window runs Python instructions immediately.

Look at my pretty shell!

The shell window

When you open IDLE, the shell window pops up. This is the best place to get started because you don't have to create a new file first. You just type the code directly into the shell window.

▽ **Working in the shell**

You can use the shell window to test out snippets of code before you add them into a bigger program. The code you type can be run right away, and any messages or "bugs" (errors) are displayed.

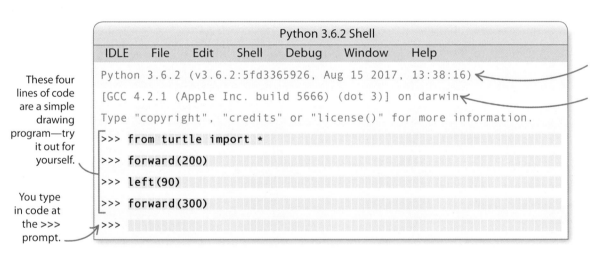

This line shows the version of Python you have.

These four lines of code are a simple drawing program—try it out for yourself.

You type in code at the >>> prompt.

```
Python 3.6.2 Shell
IDLE    File    Edit    Shell    Debug    Window    Help
Python 3.6.2 (v3.6.2:5fd3365926, Aug 15 2017, 13:38:16)
[GCC 4.2.1 (Apple Inc. build 5666) (dot 3)] on darwin
Type "copyright", "credits" or "license()" for more information.
>>> from turtle import *
>>> forward(200)
>>> left(90)
>>> forward(300)
>>>
```

The text here will depend on your operating system.

⊞ ⬝ ⬝ EXPERT TIPS

Different windows

To help you know which window you should type your code in, we've given each window in IDLE a different color.

    Shell window

    Editor window

```
>>> print("You've unlocked a new level!")
```

```
>>> 123 + 456 * (7 / 8)
```

```
>>> ''.join(reversed("Time to play"))
```

△ **Give the shell a test run**

Type each of these code snippets into the shell window and press **Enter** after each one. The first line displays a message and the second line does a calculation. Can you figure out what the third line does?

The editor window

The shell window can't save your code, so when you close it, the code you typed is gone forever. When you are working on a game, you should use IDLE's editor window. This will let you save your code. It also has built-in tools to help you write your programs and troubleshoot any errors.

▽ **The editor window**
To open the editor window in IDLE, click on the **File** menu at the top and choose **New File**. An empty editor will then appear. You'll use the editor window to write the programs for the games in this book.

You type in the code here. This program prints a list that tells you which numbers are even and which ones are odd.

The name of the file is shown here.

You can run Python programs from this menu, but you will run Pygame Zero programs a different way.

Anything you tell Python to print gets displayed in the shell window.

The menu bar for the editor window is different from the one for the shell window.

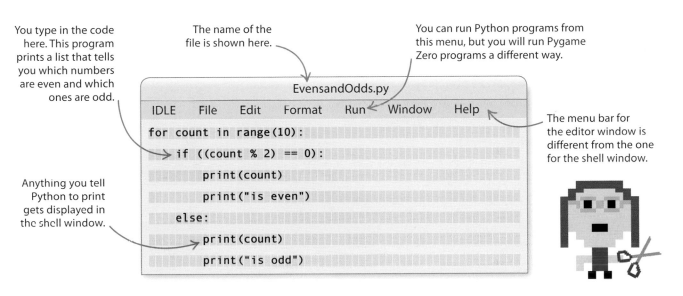

EvensandOdds.py

| IDLE | File | Edit | Format | Run | Window | Help |

```
for count in range(10):
    if ((count % 2) == 0):
        print(count)
        print("is even")
    else:
        print(count)
        print("is odd")
```

Colors in the code

IDLE automatically colors the text to highlight different parts of the code. The colors make it easier to understand the code, and they're useful when you're trying to spot mistakes.

Symbols and names
Most code text is colored black.

Built-in commands
Python commands, such as **print()**, are shown in purple.

Errors
Python uses red to alert you to any errors in your code.

Output
Any text produced when a program runs is blue.

Keywords
Certain words, such as **if** and **else**, are special Python keywords. They are shown in orange.

Text in quotation marks
Any text in quotation marks is green. These are called strings.

Your first program

After you've installed Python, Pygame, and Pygame Zero, follow these steps to write your first Python program. This simple program will display a message on the screen.

EXPERT TIPS

Type carefully

Make sure you type all your code exactly as it's written in this book. The grid will help you get it all correct. A tiny typo in just one line of code can cause a whole program to crash.

How it works

This Python program will check if everything is set up properly so you can start building some games. It uses Pygame Zero to display the word "Hello" on the screen.

1 **Set up a folder**
Before you start, create a folder called *python-games* somewhere easy to find, such as on your Desktop. Create another folder within your python-games folder and call it *hello*.

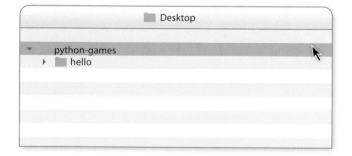

```
                    Desktop

  ▼   python-games
      ▶   hello
```

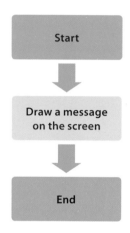

△ **Hello flowchart**
When building a game, programmers use diagrams called flowcharts to plan their game and show how it works. Each step is shown in a box, with an arrow leading to the next step. More complicated games might have steps with questions and more than one arrow leading to different boxes, depending on the answer to the question.

2 **Start IDLE**
Open IDLE on your computer. From the **File** menu, choose **New File** to create an empty editor window where you can write your program.

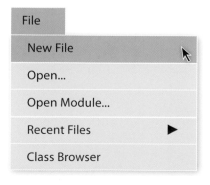

```
File

New File

Open...

Open Module...

Recent Files        ▶

Class Browser
```

3 **Type the first line of code**
Write this first line of code that tells Python to show, or "draw," something on the screen. Press **Enter** when you're done.

```
def draw():
```

This line of code is used to print something on the screen.

Here we go!

4 **Type the second line of code**
Then type in this second line of code. Check that it starts with four spaces. This is called an "indent," and your code won't work without it!

```
def draw():
    screen.draw.text("Hello", topleft=(10, 10))
```

Add four blank spaces here if IDLE hasn't done it automatically.

Make sure you have two closing parentheses here.

5 **Save the file**
Now let's save the file. Go to the **File** menu and choose **Save As...**. Name the file *hello.py* and save it in the folder you created earlier.

Save As:	hello.py
Tags:	
Where:	hello

Cancel   Save

When you save a program, IDLE adds ".py" to the end automatically, so you don't have to type it in.

Hey, grab on! I'll save you!

Running your program

Because your games use Pygame Zero, you usually have to run them in a different way from normal Python programs. It isn't difficult once you get used to it, however.

6 **Open Command Prompt or Terminal window**
To run the program, you can use the command line. If you're using a Windows computer, this is in the Command Prompt app. If you're on a Mac, open the Terminal app.

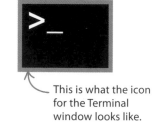

This is what the icon for Command Prompt looks like.

This is what the icon for the Terminal window looks like.

7 **Type in the Pygame Zero command**
To tell Pygame Zero to run the game, type **pgzrun** into the command line and leave a space, but don't press **Enter** yet!

🏠 Sanjay – bash – 80x24

```
Last login: Sun Sep 3 17:18:36 on ttys000
LC-0797:~ sanjay$ pgzrun
```

Don't forget to leave a space after **pgzrun**.

8 **Drag and drop the IDLE file**
Keep the app open, and using Explorer (Windows) or Finder (Mac), go to the folder where you saved your program. Once you find it, drag and drop the .py file into the command line.

🏠 Sanjay – bash – 80x24

```
Last login: Sun Sep 3 17:18:36 on ttys000
LC-0797:~ sanjay$ pgzrun User/Documents/python-games/hello.py
```

python-games

Name

▼ ▦ hello
   🐍 hello.py

Drag and drop hello.py into the Command Prompt or Terminal window.

The location of your IDLE file will appear here when you drop it in.

9 **Run the program**
Now that you've typed in the **pgzrun** command and your computer knows where to find the IDLE file, press **Enter**. This will launch Pygame Zero.

10 **Final screen**
If your program is working correctly, you'll see a window with a "Hello" message written in the top-left corner of the screen. Good job! Now it's time to become a Python games coder!

EXPERT TIPS

Rerunning programs

When you're building a program, you need to run the code frequently to check for bugs. To save time, you can press the **Up** arrow key in Command Prompt or Terminal to see your recent commands. You can then press **Enter** to run one of them again. If your game is still running, you need to close it before rerunning your code. If you don't, nothing will happen!

Running your program using IDLE

It's possible to run your Pygame Zero programs using IDLE. To do this you need to add two extra lines to your code. It's a good idea to wait until you have finish writing your program before doing this.

1 Type **import pgzrun** at the very top of your program and **pgzrun.go()** at the very end. The entire code for your game should now sit between these two lines.

2 To run the game in IDLE go to the **Run** menu and click **Run Module**, or just press the **F5** key.

This should now be the first line of your program.

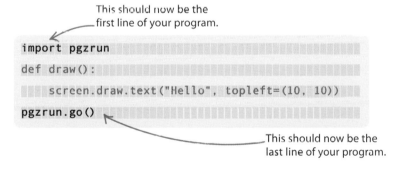

```
import pgzrun
def draw():
    screen.draw.text("Hello", topleft=(10, 10))
pgzrun.go()
```

This should now be the last line of your program.

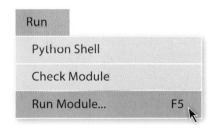

IMPORTANT!

Fix mistakes

If nothing happens when you run one of your programs, or if you get an error message—don't panic! It's normal to experience errors (these are called "bugs") when coding a program. If an error message appears, ask yourself the following questions:

- Does the code match the given example exactly?
- Have I saved the program in the right folder?
- Have I typed **pgzrun** correctly?
- Are Pygame and Pygame Zero installed correctly?

I think there's some bug spray on pages 44–47!

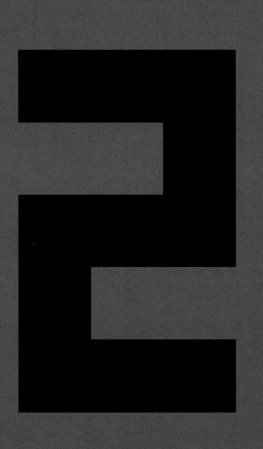

Learning
the basics

Creating variables

Variables are used to store and label pieces of information. You'll use them a lot in your code—for example, to hold your current score or keep track of how many lives you have left.

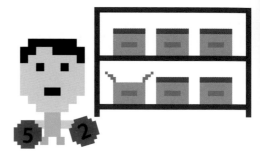

How to create a variable

You need to give each variable a name that describes what data is stored inside it. What the variable stores is called its value. Type the name followed by an equals sign, then type the value, with a space between each part. This is called "assigning a value" to the variable.

△ **Storage box**
A variable is like a box with a name label. You can store data in the box and then use its name to find the data again when you need to use it.

1 **Assign a value**
Open IDLE's shell window. Type this line of code to create a variable called **score** and assign a value to it.

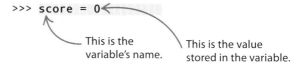

```
>>> score = 0
```

This is the variable's name.

This is the value stored in the variable.

2 **Print the value**
Now type **print(score)** into the window after the code you typed in Step 1. Press **Enter** to see what happens.

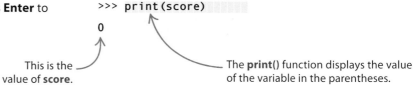

```
>>> score = 0
>>> print(score)
0
```

This is the value of **score**.

The **print()** function displays the value of the variable in the parentheses.

Naming variables

Always choose a meaningful name for each variable in your programs. For example, a variable for tracking the number of attempts a player has left could be called **attempts_remaining**, rather than just **attempts** or **a**. Variable names can contain letters, numbers, and underscores, but they should always start with a letter. Follow these rules and you won't go wrong.

Dos and don'ts
- Always start the variable's name with a letter.
- Any letter or number can be used in the name.
- Symbols such as -, /, #, @ aren't allowed.
- Do not use spaces. An underscore (_) can be used instead.
- Uppercase (capital) and lowercase letters are different. Python will treat **Score** and **score** as two different variables.
- Avoid words that are used in Python or Pygame Zero as commands, such as "function" or "screen."

Using numbers

Variables can be used to store numbers, which can then be used in calculations. You can use them with symbols, just like you do in math. Be careful with multiplication and division, though, because they use different symbols from the ones you use at school.

Symbol	Meaning
+	add
–	subtract
*	multiply
/	divide

1 **A simple calculation**
Type this code into the shell window. It uses two variables, **x** and **y**, which store integers to perform a simple calculation. Press **Enter** to see the answer.

```
>>> x = 2
>>> y = x * 3
>>> print(y)
6
```

Create a new variable, **x**, and assign the value **2** to it.

Multiply **x** by **3** and assign the result to another variable, **y**.

Print the value assigned to **y**.

The result of the calculation.

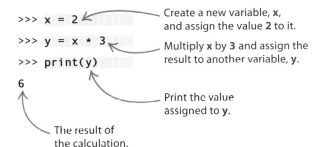

3 **Update the value**
The value of **y** needs to be updated to get the correct result. To do this, you need to run the **y = x * 3** calculation again. Now the code assigns the new value to **y** after **x** has been changed.

```
>>> x = 5
>>> y = x * 3
>>> print(y)
15
```

You need to redo the calculation to update the value of **y**.

2 **Change a value**
To change the value of a variable, just assign a new value to it. In this code, assign the value **5** to **x**. Print the value assigned to **y** again. What do you think the result will be?

```
>>> x = 5
>>> print(y)
6
```

Change the value of **x**.

The result hasn't changed—next we'll find out why.

· · · LINGO

Integers and floats

In coding, different types of numbers can be stored in variables. Whole numbers are called "integers," and numbers with a decimal point in them are called "floats." Integers are usually used to count things, like a player's score, whereas floats are usually used for measurements, such as temperature.

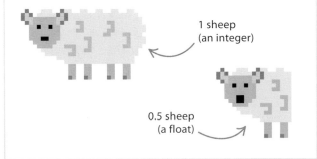

1 sheep (an integer)

0.5 sheep (a float)

Working with strings

A string is any data made up of a sequence of letters or other characters. Words and sentences are stored as strings. In Python, most programs use at least one string. Any character that you can type on your keyboard can be stored in a string.

1 Strings in variables

Strings can be assigned to variables. Type this code into the shell window. It assigns the string **Martin** to the **name** variable and then displays it. Strings must be written between quotation marks to show where they start and end.

```
>>> name = "Martin"
>>> print(name)
Martin
```

Quotation marks tell the computer that it's a string.

Press **Enter** to print the string.

2 Joining strings together

Variables can be combined to create new ones. For example, you can add two strings and store the combination in a new variable. Type this code into the shell window to try this out. You can change the greeting and the name to make a new message.

Remember the quotation marks, and leave a space after **Hello**.

Remember the space after the greeting.

```
>>> greeting = "Hello "
>>> name = "Martin"
>>> message = greeting + name
>>> print(message)
Hello Martin
```

message is a new variable that contains the **greeting** and **name** variables.

The + symbol can be used to join strings together.

EXPERT TIPS

Length of a string

For some programs, it's useful to be able to count the number of characters in a string. You can do this using the function **len()**. A function is a useful operation that contains multiple lines of code, so you don't have to enter them manually. To find out the number of characters in the string **Hello Martin**, type this line of code into the shell after you've created the string, then hit **Enter**.

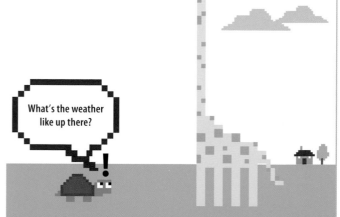

What's the weather like up there?

The number of characters, including spaces, is counted.

```
>>> len(message)
12
```

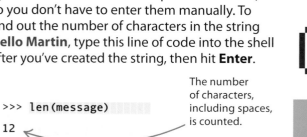

Making lists

A list is used to store a collection of data. It can hold many different values and keep them in order. For example, a list can store a deck of cards for a game, such as Snap, so the code knows which card to deal next. The position of each value in the list is identified with a number, starting from 0. You can use these numbers to change list values.

1 **More than one variable**

Imagine you're coding a multiplayer game and want to have a different variable for each card. You would need 52 variables to store a whole deck of cards, but we'll just work with six for now.

```
>>> card1 = "1 hearts"
>>> card2 = "2 hearts"
>>> card3 = "3 hearts"
>>> card4 = "4 hearts"
>>> card5 = "5 hearts"
>>> card6 = "6 hearts"
```

There's no need to type this code out.

2 **List in a variable**

It would be much easier to use a list to store all the values of the cards instead of setting up so many variables individually. To create a list, surround the values you want to store with square brackets.

The values must be separated by commas.

```
>>> cards = ["1 hearts", "2 hearts", "3 hearts", "4 hearts", "5 hearts", "6 hearts"]
```

The list is assigned to the variable **cards**.

3 **Getting items from a list**

It's easy to work with a list once you have all your values in it. To get an item from a list, type the name of the list, followed by the item's position in the list within square parentheses. But watch out—in Python, the first position in a list is 0, not 1. Now try getting different cards out of your **cards** list.

This line gets the first value in the list.

```
>>> cards[0]
>>> "1 hearts"
>>> cards[5]
>>> "6 hearts"
```

For our small list, the last position is 5, but for the entire **cards** list it would be 51.

This is the last value in our list.

Making decisions

Playing a game involves making decisions about what to do next. These are often based on answers to questions. For example, "Do I have any lives left?"; "Is someone chasing me?"; "Have I beaten the highest score?"

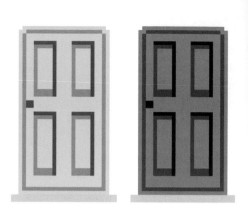

Comparisons

Computers also make decisions about what to do next by asking questions. These questions usually involve comparing two values. For instance, is one number bigger than the other? If it is, the computer might skip a block of code that it would otherwise have run.

Which door should we go through?

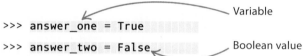
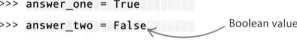

```
>>> answer_one = True
>>> answer_two = False
```

Variable

Boolean value

△ **Boolean values**

The questions that computers ask only have two possible answers: True or False. Python calls these two values Boolean values, and they must always start with a capital letter. You can store a Boolean value in a variable.

Symbol	Meaning
==	equal to
!=	not equal to
<	less than
>	greater than

△ **Logical operators**

The symbols and words shown here are called "logical operators," and they help computers make comparisons in order to ask questions.

Equals signs

In Python, there are two types of equals sign: a single equals sign = and a double equals sign ==. These signs have different meanings. You use a single equals sign when you want to store a value in a variable. For example, **lives = 10** stores the value **10** in the variable **lives**. However, use a double equals sign when you want to compare two values.

This sets the value of the variable.

This compares your age with the variable.

```
>>> age = 10
>>> if age == 10:
        print("You are ten years old.")
```

The code prints the message if the two match.

Monsters and coins

Let's try an example in the shell window. You can use the variables **monsters** and **coins** to represent three monsters and four coins, respectively. Type in the following code.

```
>>> monsters = 3
>>> coins = 4
```

This value is stored in the variable **monsters**.

This variable stores the number of coins.

▽ **Let's compare**

Now type the following lines of code to compare the values in the two variables. After typing each line, press **Enter** and Python will tell you if the statements are True or False.

```
>>> coins > monsters
True
```

This expression is True because the number of coins is greater than the number of monsters.

```
>>> monsters == coins
False
```

This expression is False because the number of monsters and the number of coins aren't equal.

```
>>> monsters < coins
True
```

This expression is True because the number of monsters is less than the number of coins.

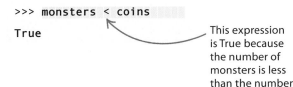

Boolean expressions

Statements that contain variables and values and use logical operators always give you a Boolean value—True or False. Because of this, these statements are called Boolean expressions. All of the statements about monsters and coins in the examples are Boolean expressions.

coins is a variable.

```
>>> coins > monsters
True
```

monsters is a variable.

True is a Boolean value.

> is a logical operator.

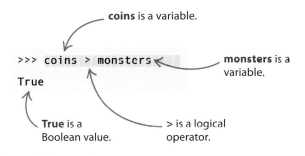

▽ **Multiple comparisons**

In Python, you can also combine more than one comparison by using the logical operators **and** and **or**.

```
>>> (monsters == 3) and (coins == 4)
True
```

When using **and**, both the comparisons need to be correct for the Boolean value to be True.

When using **or**, only one of the comparisons needs to be correct for the Boolean value to be True.

```
>>> (monsters == 7) or (coins == 4)
True
```

Level up

Imagine you're creating a game that has two levels. To get to Level 2, you need to have at least four magic snails and a score of more than 100 points. At this point, you have 110 points but only three magic snails. Use the shell window to see if you can still get to Level 2. First, create variables for the score and number of snails collected and assign the correct values to them. Then type the rules for getting to Level 2 as a Boolean expression.

Store values in variables.

```
>>> score = 110
>>> snails = 3
>>> (score > 100) and (snails >= 4)
False
```

This is a Boolean expression meaning "score greater than 100 and snails more than or equal to 4."

This shows you cannot progress to Level 2 yet.

Branching

Sometimes you need to make decisions when playing a game. Should you turn right to investigate the library or turn left to look at the kitchen? Computer programs often contain code that runs only in certain situations. This means the computer makes decisions about which parts of the code to run.

◁ **Eye on the ball**

Imagine you're playing a soccer game and you need to decide which way to aim the ball at the goal. You could ask yourself, "Is the goalkeeper near the left side of the goal?" If he is, you aim at the right side of the goal. If he isn't, you aim left. In Python, the different routes through a program lead to different blocks of code. The computer uses a Boolean expression, or a condition, to decide which blocks to run.

▽ One branch

The simplest type of branching command is an **if** statement. It only has one branch, which the computer takes if the condition is True.

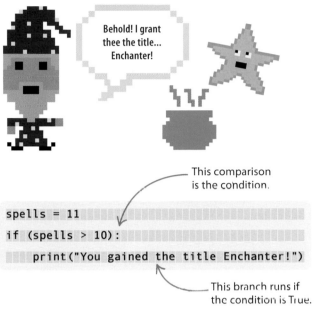

This comparison is the condition.

```
spells = 11
if (spells > 10):
    print("You gained the title Enchanter!")
```

This branch runs if the condition is True.

How it works

In this example, the program checks to see the number of spells you've cast. If it's more than ten, the program prints "You gained the title Enchanter!" If the number of spells you've cast is less than ten, the message is not printed.

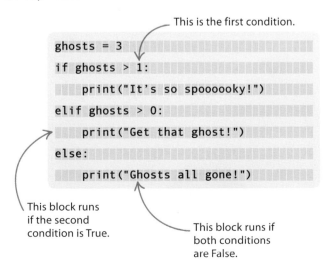

This is the first condition.

```
ghosts = 3
if ghosts > 1:
    print("It's so spooooooky!")
elif ghosts > 0:
    print("Get that ghost!")
else:
    print("Ghosts all gone!")
```

This block runs if the second condition is True.

This block runs if both conditions are False.

▽ Two branches

What if you want the program to do one thing if a condition is True, but another if it's False? In this case, you need a command with two possible branches, called an **if-else** statement.

```
game_over = True
if game_over:
    print("Game Over!")
else:
    print("Keep playing!")
```

This block runs if the condition is False.

How it works

In this example, there's a variable called **game_over**, which is set to True. The **if** statement checks to see if **game_over** is True. If it is, the program prints "Game Over!" If it isn't, the **else** statement runs to print "Keep playing!" Try running this code with **game_over** set to True, then False, to see this in action.

GAME OVER

◁ More than two branches

When there are more than two possible paths, the command **elif** (short for "else-if") can be used in your program. In the following example, you need to capture several ghosts in one go.

How it works

In this program, the variable **ghosts** has been set to **3**, so the first branch is True and the program prints "It's so spooooooky!" But if the value in **ghosts** was 1, the first branch would be False, so the second branch would run, printing "Get that ghost!" If neither of the above branches are True, the program moves on to the third branch to print "Ghosts all gone!" An **elif** statement must always come after **if** and before **else**.

Playing with loops

When you're coding a game, you often need to run the same bit of code several times, but it would be pretty boring if you had to type it in every single time. Luckily, you can use a loop to run the same block of code over and over again. There are many different types of loops.

"For" loops

When you know exactly how many times you want a loop to repeat, you can use a **for** loop. In this example, the code prints "You are the high scorer!" ten times. Try out the code for yourself in the shell window.

```
>>> for count in range(1, 11):
        print("You are the high scorer!")
```

This is the loop variable.

The code that gets repeated is known as the "loop body."

Loop variable

The loop variable keeps track of how many times the loop has run so far. At the start of the loop, it's equal to the first number in the range. The second time around, it's equal to the second number in the range, and so on. Once it completes the second-to-last number in the range, the loop stops.

How are you doing that?

EXPERT TIPS

Range

In Python, the word **range** followed by two numbers in parentheses stands for "all the numbers in the list from the first number to the second-to-the-last number." Therefore, **range(1, 5)** contains the numbers 1, 2, 3, and 4, but not 5, so the loop runs four times.

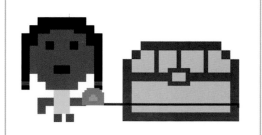

Loop body

The block of code that gets repeated in a loop is called the loop body. You must always indent the commands in the body four spaces from the beginning of the line that starts the **for** loop.

Page 31 will help you out with lists.

Looping over a list

Gaming programs often use a collection of items grouped together in a list. If you want to do something with each item on the list, you can use a **for** loop.

Listing robots

In this example, there is a list that contains the names of three robots that the player has to escape from in a game.

Python will add one of the robots' names here.

```
>>> robots = ["Bing", "Bleep", "Bloop"]
>>> for robot in robots:
        print("I am a robot. My name is " + robot)
```

robot is a temporary variable that moves along the **robots** list each time the loop runs.

How it works

We create a temporary variable called **robot** that holds a single item in the list. The value in **robot** is updated each time around the loop, so that it holds Bing, then Bleep, and finally Bloop. Once it reaches the end of the list, the loop stops.

Looping over two lists

Python can loop through a list from start to finish more or less automatically. But if you want to loop through two lists at once, you need to use an extra variable to tell Python to move through both lists.

Robots with colors

In this example, we have two lists. One is called **robots** and holds the names of the robots. The other is called **colors** and tells you the color of each robot. This program uses a variable called **index** to move through both lists, printing out each robot's name and also what color it is.

The **index** variable keeps track of the position each list is at.

index will help Python move through both lists in order.

This line updates **index** so Python moves through the lists with each loop.

```
>>> robots = ["Bing", "Bleep", "Bloop"]
>>> colors = ["red", "orange", "purple"]
>>> index = 0
>>> for each in robots:
        print("My name is " + robots[index] + ". I am " + colors[index])
        index = index + 1
```

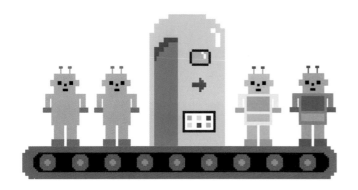

How it works

robots[index] and **colors[index]** both use the value of **index** to decide which item in their list to print. Since **index** is set to **0** to begin with, both lists will start with the first item—remember the first position in Python lists is always 0, not 1. Since Bing is at position **0** of the list **robots** and red is at position **0** of the list **colors**, that means Bing is red. Each time the loop runs, it adds 1 to **index**, moving each list onto the next item, so Bleep will be orange and Bloop will be purple. The loop will continue until it reaches the end of the lists.

"While" loops

Sometimes, while coding a program, you might not know exactly how many times you want a loop to repeat. Don't worry! In this case, you can use a **while** loop.

Loop condition

A **while** loop includes a question whose answer can either be True or False. This is called a loop condition. The **while** loop will only start if the answer to the loop condition is True. Imagine you are playing a game where a castle is guarded by a dragon that checks if you have the magic key. "Do you have the magic key?" would be the loop condition and the castle would be the loop body. If you have the magic key, the loop condition is True and you can enter the castle. But if you don't have the key, the loop condition is False, so you can't get into the loop!

EXPERT TIPS

Indentation error

Just like the **for** loop, the code in the body of a **while** loop must be four spaces further in than the line starting the loop. If you don't do this, Python will show an error message saying "unexpected indent."

Nobody enters without the magic key!

Balloon fight

In this example, the program asks if you want to throw a water balloon. If your answer is **y**, it prints "Splash!!!" and asks if you want to throw another balloon. If your answer is **n**, the program prints "Goodbye!" and ends.

This line gets the value of **answer** (used in loop condition).

```
answer = input("Throw a water balloon? (y/n)")
while answer == "y":
    print("Splash!!!")
    answer = input("Throw another water balloon? (y/n)")
print("Goodbye!")
```

When the loop is complete, this line prints "Goodbye!"

This line gets the new value of **answer** (used in loop condition).

It's really wet in here!

How it works

The loop condition here is **answer** == "**y**", which means you want to throw a water balloon. The loop body prints "Splash!!!" to show a balloon being thrown and asks if you want to throw another. If your answer is **y**, the loop condition is True again and the loop is repeated. If your answer is **n** (or anything other than **y**), the loop condition is False and the program exits the loop and prints "Goodbye!" before ending.

Infinite loops

Sometimes, you might want a loop to repeat as long as the program is running. This can be done with an infinite loop. You can make an infinite loop by setting the loop condition to True, so that it keeps repeating a block of code forever!

```
>>> while True:
        print("This is an infinite loop!")
```

There is no False option to escape the loop.

They got away!

Making an escape

If you don't want to run an infinite loop, it's important to make sure the body of a **while** loop does something that could make the loop condition False. But don't worry if you accidentally code a program with an infinite loop—you can escape it by holding down the **Ctrl** key and pressing the **C** key along with it.

Functions

Functions are really handy tools for all coders. They let you name useful chunks of code so that you can use them over and over again without having to type the whole thing out each time—you just have to type in the name! Python comes with some built-in functions, but you can also write your own to handle tasks specific to your games.

Using functions

When you want to use one of Python's built-in functions, all you need to do is "call" it by typing out its name followed by a pair of empty parentheses. This tells Python to run the code saved in that function. If you need to give a function some data to use, it goes inside the parentheses. This is called a "parameter."

Built-in functions

Python comes with a number of built-in functions. They allow you to perform a variety of tasks, from printing messages to converting one type of data to another.

This calls the **print()** function with a string parameter.

```
>>> print("This is a parameter")
This is a parameter
```

The string parameter is printed.

△ **print()**
One of the most commonly used functions is **print()**. This function lets you display a string (a series of letters, numbers, or other characters) on the screen. The string is a parameter in this case.

I need to build this very carefully!

▷ input()

This function lets the player enter information for the game to use, rather than the coder putting it in the original code. For example, imagine you're creating a game and you want to create a variable to store the player's name, but you don't know what they're called. You can use **input()** to make the game ask the player what their name is. Their answer becomes a return value, which the function will then assign to the **name** variable.

This is a variable that will later store the player's name.

input() asks the user what their name is.

```
>>> name = input("What is your name?")
What is your name?Ben
>>> print(name)
Ben
```

You can type your own name in here.

input() has assigned the answer to the **name** variable.

Another way to call functions

Some types of data, such as integers and strings, have their own built-in functions that are used to manipulate or change that data. These are known as "member" functions and can be called by placing a dot immediately after the data, followed by the name of the function and a pair of parentheses. Try these out in the shell window.

```
>>> "functions are fun".count("fun")
2
```

The string **fun** appears twice.

△ count()

This function is used with strings. It is called on one string, with another string as a parameter of the function **count()**. The return value tells you how many times the second string appears in the first string.

```
>>> "blue".upper()
'BLUE'
```

This is the new string, all in capitals.

△ upper()

This function takes an existing string and returns a new string, replacing all the lowercase letters with uppercase (capital) letters.

A list of numbers is assigned to a variable.

The reverse function is called on the list of numbers.

```
>>> countdown = [1, 2, 3]
>>> countdown.reverse()
>>> print(countdown)
[3, 2, 1]
```

△ reverse()

You can also call a member function on a variable. In this example, the function **reverse()** is used to reverse the order of the list of numbers stored in the variable **countdown**.

The function has two parameters, which are separated by a comma.

```
>>> message = "Coding makes me happy"
>>> message.replace("happy", ":D")
'Coding makes me :D'
```

△ replace()

For this function, you need two parameters—the first is the part of a string you want to replace, and the second is what you want to replace it with. The function returns a new string with the replacement made.

Making your own functions

There isn't a built-in function for everything, so you need to know how to write, or "define," your own. A function should have one clear purpose and a name that describes what it does. Follow these steps to create a function that calculates a player's score.

1 **Define the function**
Let's create a function to keep score in a game. Open an editor window in IDLE and save it as *functions.py*. Then type in the code below, making sure you get all the indents right. After each step, save the file, go to the **Run** menu, and click **Run Module**.

EXPERT TIPS

Naming your functions

It's important to give your functions accurate names that explain what they do. This will help you understand the code. Names can contain letters, numbers, and underscores, but they should always begin with a letter. You can't use spaces, so if there are multiple words in the name of your function, separate them by using underscores instead. For example, if you were creating a function to end the game, you could name it **game_over()**.

Use the **def** keyword to define a function.

```
def fruit_score():
    print(10)

fruit_score()
```

This function doesn't take a parameter.

This is the code you're storing in the function.

This calls the function, running the code you've stored in it.

```
10
```

The score is displayed in the shell.

2 **Add some parameters**
The function works well so far, but what if you want to have different scores for different fruits you collect? For the function to know which score to print, it needs to know which fruit you have collected. Imagine you get ten points for an apple, but five points for an orange. You can do this by adding a parameter to the function.

The function now takes a parameter.

```
def fruit_score(fruit):
    if fruit == "apple":
        print(10)
    elif fruit == "orange":
        print(5)

fruit_score("apple")
fruit_score("orange")
```

These lines give a value to the parameter.

The function is called twice—once with each parameter.

```
10
5
```

The score that gets printed depends on whether the parameter is **apple** or **orange**.

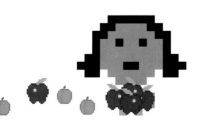

3 **Return a value**

Rather than printing out the score, you might want to use it elsewhere in your code. You can ask to get a value out of a function to be used later. This is called "returning" a value. Type in the keyword **return** before the value you want it to return in each case. Try switching your **print** statements to **return** statements.

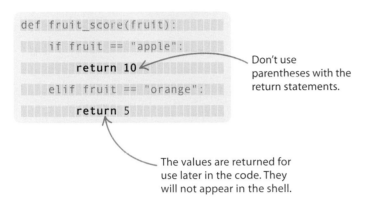

```
def fruit_score(fruit):
    if fruit == "apple":
        return 10
    elif fruit == "orange":
        return 5
```

Don't use parentheses with the return statements.

The values are returned for use later in the code. They will not appear in the shell.

Indentation Errors

Python uses indentation to understand where a block of code starts and stops. An "IndentationError" appears when something is wrong with the way you've structured the code. Remember that if a line of code ends with a colon (:), the next line needs to be indented. If Python does not add them automatically, use the **Space bar** to manually insert four spaces.

Error... error!

4 **Using the return value**

You can use the return value of a function elsewhere in your code. In this case, we make two calls to the function—one for each fruit. We then add these results together to get a total score. Add this code underneath what you wrote in Step 3 and then go to the **Run** menu and click **Run Module**.

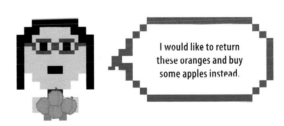

I would like to return these oranges and buy some apples instead.

```
return 5

apple_score = fruit_score("apple")
orange_score = fruit_score("orange")

total = fruit_score("apple") + fruit_score("orange")
print(total)
```

The two return values are added together.

Fixing bugs

If there's an error, or a "bug," in your code,
Python will show an error message. These
messages can be a bit confusing sometimes,
but they tell you what is wrong with your
code and how to fix it.

Help me find
those delicious bugs!

Error alert

In IDLE, both the editor and shell windows
can display an error message when something
unexpected happens. This message highlights
the error and shows you which line of code
to find it in.

▽ **Messages in Command Prompt/Terminal**
Error messages in Pygame Zero are shown in
the Command Prompt or Terminal window.
When an error is discovered, the program will
stop running and will tell you what the error is
and where to look for it in the code.

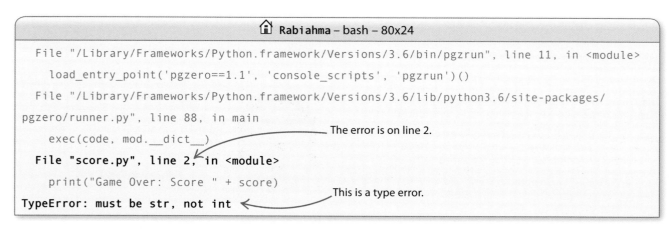

⌂ Rabiahma – bash – 80x24

```
  File "/Library/Frameworks/Python.framework/Versions/3.6/bin/pgzrun", line 11, in <module>
    load_entry_point('pgzero==1.1', 'console_scripts', 'pgzrun')()
  File "/Library/Frameworks/Python.framework/Versions/3.6/lib/python3.6/site-packages/
pgzero/runner.py", line 88, in main
    exec(code, mod.__dict__)
  File "score.py", line 2, in <module>
    print("Game Over: Score " + score)
TypeError: must be str, not int
```

The error is on line 2.

This is a type error.

... **EXPERT TIPS**

Catching bugs

When you see an error in the Command
Prompt (Windows) or Terminal (Mac), look at
the line number. Go back to your code in
IDLE and click anywhere in the file. The line
number will be displayed at the bottom-
right corner of the screen—for example,
Ln: 12. Then use the **Up** or **Down** arrow
to find the line with the error in it.

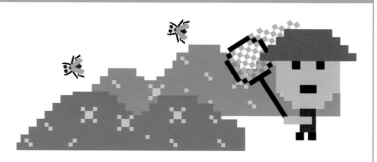

Syntax errors

The structure of statements used in a coding language is known as syntax. A syntax error means that you've typed something wrong. You could have missed a part of a statement or misspelled a word. Syntax errors are the easiest mistakes to fix. Go to the line with the error and change what you've mistyped.

▷ **Mistakes to watch out for**

Do your opening and closing parentheses match? Are you missing a quotation mark? Have you spelled everything correctly? These are the main causes of syntax errors.

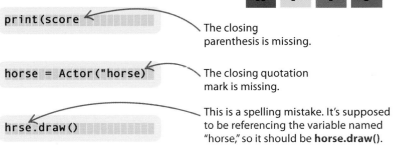

```
print(score
```
The closing parenthesis is missing.

```
horse = Actor("horse)
```
The closing quotation mark is missing.

```
hrse.draw()
```
This is a spelling mistake. It's supposed to be referencing the variable named "horse," so it should be **horse.draw()**.

Indentation errors

Python uses indentation to show where blocks of code begin and end. Indentation errors are displayed if you make a mistake with the structure of the code. If a line of code ends with a colon, you must indent the next line. Python automatically indents after colons, but you can also do it manually by adding four spaces.

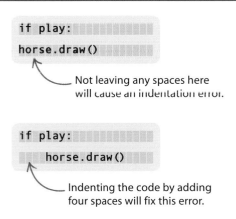

```
if play:
horse.draw()
```
Not leaving any spaces here will cause an indentation error.

```
if play:
    horse.draw()
```
Indenting the code by adding four spaces will fix this error.

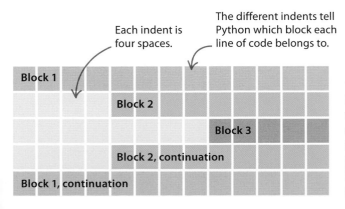

Each indent is four spaces.

The different indents tell Python which block each line of code belongs to.

Block 1
Block 2
Block 3
Block 2, continuation
Block 1, continuation

◁ **Indent each new block**

Python programs usually have blocks of code within other blocks, such as an **if** statement inside a loop. Every line in a block must be indented by the same amount. This can be done for each indent by pressing the **Space bar** four times. Even though Python automatically indents after colons, you should get used to checking if the indentation is correct.

Type errors

These errors occur when you put the wrong type of data in the code. For example, if the code is expecting a number but you give it a string, it won't work.

Sigh! I really thought it would work.

```
lives_remaining = lives_remaining - "one"
```

This keeps track of the number of lives a player is left with.

lives_remaining stores whole numbers, or integers, so it doesn't make sense to minus the string **"one"** from it. You need to use the digit **1** instead.

```
score = 100 > "high_score"
```

It doesn't make sense to check if a number is greater than a string, because they are different data types.

Removing the quotation marks around **high_score** would make this code work properly.

```
players = ["Martin", "Craig", "Claire", "Daniel"]
find_highest_score(players)
```

This function expects a list of integers, but instead it has been assigned a list of strings representing players' names.

◁ **Examples of type errors**

Type errors occur when you code something that doesn't make sense. Subtracting a string from a number, comparing different data types, or trying to find the highest number in a list of strings are all type errors.

Can you make a web out of these pineapples?

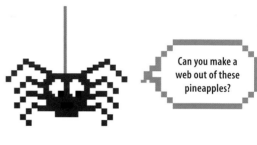

Name errors

A name error occurs when you try to use a variable or function that hasn't been created yet. To avoid this, you must remember to define all variables and functions before using them.

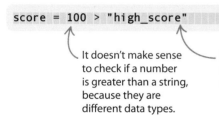

Is this a date?

No, it's a pear.

▷ **Example of a name error**

This code will give you a name error if you try to display the contents of a variable before creating it. Remember, you need to create the variable first.

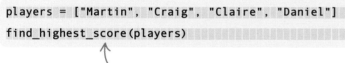

```
print("Welcome " + player_name)
player_name = "Martin"
```

You need to assign **"Martin"** to the variable **player_name** first.

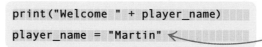

Logic errors

Sometimes you may not get any error messages, but your code still won't work the way you want it to. This is because, as far as Python is concerned, there's nothing wrong with the program, but the logic of the code is incorrect. This is called a logic error. You might have missed an important line of code, or maybe you've put in the right instructions but in the wrong order.

```
2 X 2 = 4
2 X 3 = 6
2 X 4 = 8
2 X 5 = 10
6 X 2 = 12
```

Something isn't quite right! I can feel it.

```
print("You lost a life!")
print(lives)
lives = lives - 1
```

There are no errors in the code, but the last two lines are in the wrong order.

◁ **Can you spot the bug?**

This code will run with no error messages, but it contains a logic error. When the player loses a life, the value of **lives** is shown on the screen before the number of lives is reduced by one. That means the player will see the wrong number of lives remaining! To fix it, you'd have to move the instruction **print(lives)** to the end.

▷ **Fixing logic**

Logic errors can be the hardest to find and fix. You can only get better at it with more experience. To make logic errors easier to find, run your code frequently to test it. If you think there is an error, go through each line of code carefully. For example, when checking the value assigned to a variable at different stages in the program, try using a **print()** statement to spot any errors.

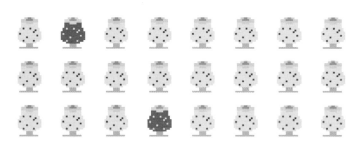

Bug-busting checklist

Coding can get frustrating sometimes, and you might feel as if you'll never be able to find a solution. But don't give up! If you follow the tips in this handy checklist, you'll be able to identify most errors.

Should I be worried?

Ask yourself...

- Have you typed the code exactly as it is in the book? Pay extra attention to indentation and spaces.
- Is everything spelled correctly?
- Do you have extra spaces at the start of a line?
- Have you confused any numbers for letters, such as 0 and O?
- Have you used the correct case for all the letters?
- Do opening parentheses have a matching closing parenthesis? () [] {}
- Does every quotation mark have a matching closing quotation mark?
- Have you asked someone else to check your code for you and compare it with the book?
- Have you saved your code since you last made changes?

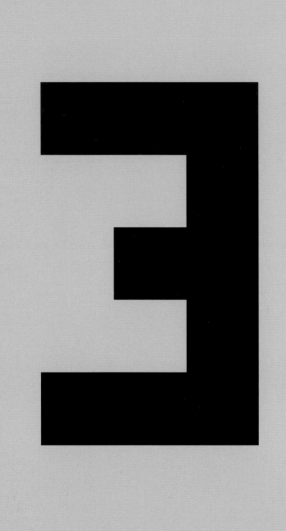

Shoot the Fruit

How to build Shoot the Fruit

This simple shooting game is a fun way to practice your aim. When the apple appears, click on it to "shoot" it. Aim carefully though, because if you miss, the game is over!

What happens

When the game starts, an apple appears on the screen for you to "shoot." If you hit it, a "Good shot!" message pops up, and the apple appears at another point on the screen. But if you miss, a "You missed!" message is shown, and the game ends.

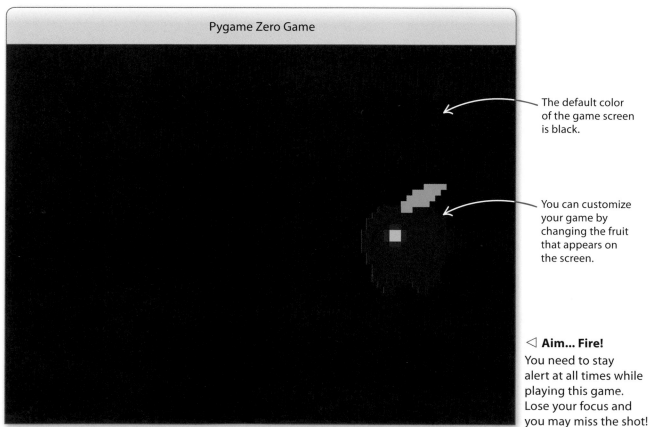

Pygame Zero Game

The default color of the game screen is black.

You can customize your game by changing the fruit that appears on the screen.

◁ **Aim... Fire!**
You need to stay alert at all times while playing this game. Lose your focus and you may miss the shot!

How it works

The game is constantly checking whether you've clicked the mouse button. Every time you click on the apple, it needs to be drawn again somewhere else on the screen. If you click and miss, the game will end.

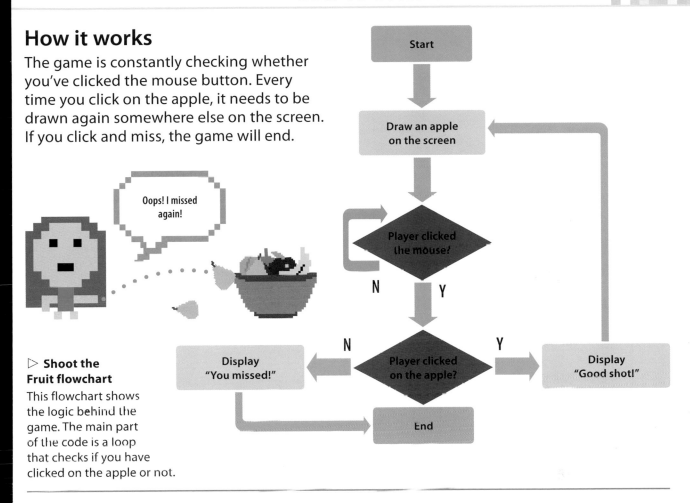

▷ **Shoot the Fruit flowchart**

This flowchart shows the logic behind the game. The main part of the code is a loop that checks if you have clicked on the apple or not.

Get shooting!

Are you ready to code? In this program, you'll start by drawing an apple on the screen, then you'll learn to place it at random points before you start shooting it. Ready? Let's get coding!

1 **Open IDLE**
Create an empty file in IDLE by going to the **File** menu and choosing **New File**.

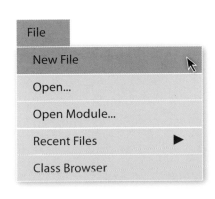

2 **Save your game**
Go to the **File** menu and click **Save As...**. Then save your program in the python-games folder. Create this folder now if you haven't made it already. Inside this folder, make another folder called *shoot-the-fruit* and save your IDLE file in it as *shoot.py*.

Save As:	shoot.py
Tags:	
Where:	shoot-the-fruit

Cancel   Save

3 **Set up an image folder**
This game uses an image of an apple. Within your shoot-the-fruit folder, right-click and choose **New Folder** to create another folder and call it *images*. It needs to be in the same place as your IDLE file.

New Folder

Get Info

Clean up

Clean up by ▶

4 **Put the image into the folder**
Go to **dk.com/computercoding** and download the Python Games Resource Pack or just the Shoot the Fruit images. Find the file called "apple.png". Copy this file into the images folder. Your folders should look something like this now.

shoot-the-fruit
- shoot.py
- ▼ images
  - apple.png

5 **Introducing an Actor**
Now you can start writing some code. Go back to IDLE and write this line of code in the editor window, then press **Enter**.

```
apple = Actor("apple")
```

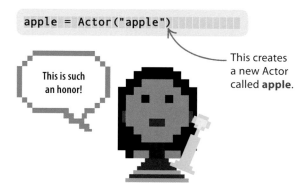

This is such an honor!

This creates a new Actor called **apple**.

I wish my folders were more organized.

⋯ LINGO

Actors and Sprites

In computer games development, a sprite is an object, like a coin or an enemy character, that is controlled by code. Actors in Python are like Sprites in Scratch. An Actor can be drawn on the screen, moved around, and even interact with other Actors in the game. Each Actor is given a "script" (the Python code) to tell it how to behave in the game.

6 Drawing the apple on the screen

Next you need to "draw" the apple on the screen. To do this, you can use a built-in Pygame Zero function called **draw()**. This function is used to redraw the game screen. For example, if a character has moved or a score has changed, you can use this function to update the screen with those changes. Write this code beneath your previous code.

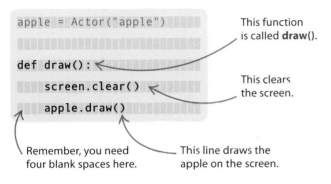

```
apple = Actor("apple")

def draw():
    screen.clear()
    apple.draw()
```

This function is called **draw()**.

This clears the screen.

Remember, you need four blank spaces here.

This line draws the apple on the screen.

7 Test the code

Now it's time to test the code. Run the program by using the command line in the Command Prompt or Terminal window. Check out pages 24–25 if you need to remind yourself how to do this.

```
pgzrun
```

Drag and drop your shoot.py file here to run it.

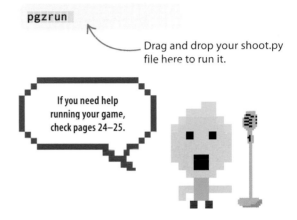

If you need help running your game, check pages 24–25.

8 First screen

If your code is working properly, you should see this screen. If it's not, or if you get an error message, go back and check your code to find any bugs.

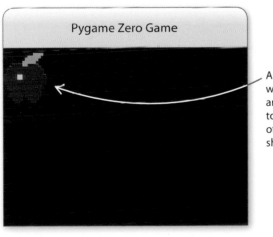

Pygame Zero Game

A blank game window with an apple in the top-left corner of the screen should appear.

9 Placing the apple

At the moment, the apple appears in the top-left corner of the game window. You can change the code to place the apple exactly where you want it on the screen. Write this function, which will place the apple at the coordinates (300, 200).

```
apple.draw()

def place_apple():
    apple.x = 300
    apple.y = 200
```

The apple will be placed 300 pixels along the x-axis (horizontal).

The apple will be placed 200 pixels down the y-axis (vertical).

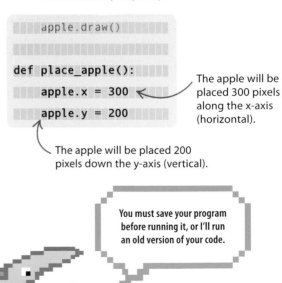

You must save your program before running it, or I'll run an old version of your code.

EXPERT TIPS
Graphics in Pygame

Python uses coordinates to identify all the places in a window where an object could be. This means that every place can be identified by using two numbers. The first number is the x coordinate, which shows how far to the right an object is. The second number is the y coordinate, which shows how far down the object is. Coordinates are written in parentheses, with the x coordinate first, like this: (x, y). In math, the coordinate (0, 0) is usually at the bottom left, but in computer graphics, it's almost always the top left.

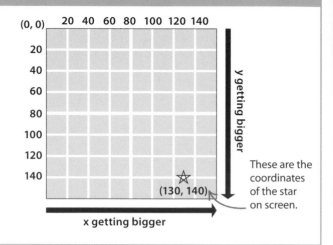

These are the coordinates of the star on screen.

x getting bigger

10 Running the function
After you've written the function to place the apple on the screen, you need to tell Python to run it. Add this extra line of code to run the function called **place_apple()**.

```
def place_apple():
    apple.x = 300
    apple.y = 200

place_apple()
```

This function places the apple at coordinates (300, 200).

11 Test it again
Save your file and then run the code from the command line. Remember, you can press the **Up** arrow in the command line to quickly choose a previous command, then press **Enter**. This time the apple will appear at the point (300, 200).

The apple is placed at coordinates (300, 200).

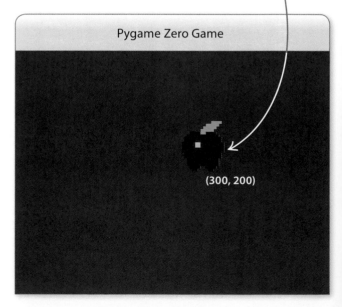

Pygame Zero Game

(300, 200)

Run fast or we'll miss the bus!

12 **Dealing with clicks**

Now it's time to write the code that will run when you press the mouse. Pygame Zero has a built-in function called **on_mouse_down()**, which is run every time you click the mouse. Type this code in between the code you added in Step 9 and Step 10, then run it from the command line. You should see the message "Good shot!" in the Command Prompt or Terminal window each time you click the mouse.

```
def place_apple():
    apple.x = 300
    apple.y = 200


def on_mouse_down(pos):
    print("Good shot!")
    place_apple()


place_apple()
```

Programmers sometimes add blank lines to make their code neater, but they aren't necessary. Python ignores blank lines completely.

13 **Adding some logic**

At this point, the "Good shot!" message is displayed every time you click the mouse, but we only want it to show if the player actually hits the apple. You can do this by amending the code from Steps 10 and 12 to include an **if** statement. This code checks if the apple and the mouse cursor are in the same position. If they are, the message is displayed.

pos is the position of the cursor when you click the mouse.

```
def on_mouse_down(pos):
    if apple.collidepoint(pos):
        print("Good shot!")
        place_apple()
```

Make sure the bottom two lines now start with eight spaces.

This function checks if the cursor is in the same position as the apple.

Whoa! Good shot!

Indents

Python uses indents to separate different blocks of code. If your indents are wrong, Python won't know how to read your code, and you'll end up with a bug! Each indent is made up of four spaces, and code can be indented more than once—for example, by eight spaces. Sometimes IDLE adds the indents for you, but if you're moving the code around, like in Step 13, you might need to indent it yourself. You can do this by entering the correct number of spaces.

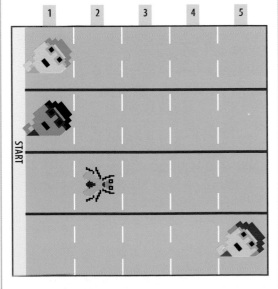

14 **Missed a shot? Game over!**
Add some more logic to your code, so that if you miss a shot and don't click on the apple, it quits the game. Try it out!

```
if apple.collidepoint(pos):
    print("Good shot!")
    place_apple()
else:
    print("You missed!")
    quit()
```

This command quits the game by stopping the program completely.

15 **Importing Random**
The game is very easy at this point, because the apple is always drawn at the same place on the screen. You can use Python's Random module to make the game more challenging by placing the apple at a random point on the screen each time it is drawn. First, add this code at the very top of your program.

```
from random import randint
apple = Actor("apple")
```

This imports the function **randint()** from Python's Random module.

16 **Using Random**
Change the code you typed in Step 9 to look like this. The code will now use the **randint()** function to pick a random number between 10 and 800 for the x coordinate and a random number between 10 and 600 for the y coordinate.

```
def place_apple():
    apple.x = randint(10, 800)
    apple.y = randint(10, 600)
```

This function picks a random number for each coordinate.

17 **Time to shoot!**
You did it! Run your program to play the game. Each time you "shoot" the apple, it will move to a random place on the screen for you to "shoot" again.

I sure have good aim!

EXPERT TIPS
Random numbers

Rolling a dice, picking a card from a deck, or tossing a coin are all actions that you can simulate by generating a random number. You can read more about how to use Python's Random module by going to the **Help** menu and clicking **Python Docs**.

Pick a card, any card.

Hacks and tweaks

Now that you've created your first game, it's time to think about how you can change it to make the game even more fun. Here are some hacks and tweaks for you to play around with.

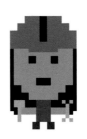

```
kiwi = Actor("kiwi")
```

△ Fruit salad

The Actor doesn't need to be an apple! Find a picture of another fruit in the Python Games Resource Pack or create one using an 8-bit editor online. Make sure you've got a suitably sized image before you save it in the images folder. Then name the image and change the code accordingly to use the new fruit as an Actor.

Page 28 will help you with the variable!

△ Keep count

Change your code so that it can keep count of the number of times you click successfully. Here are some hints to help you out.

- Store the count in a variable.
- Start by setting the variable to **0**.
- Increase the count by 1 each time you click on the apple.
- Use **print()** to show the score in the Command Prompt or Terminal window each time the apple is drawn on the screen.

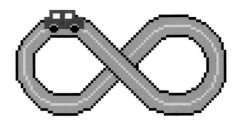

△ Keep on playing

This game is fun for people who want to practice using a mouse. However, it could get frustrating if the game quits every time you click in the wrong place. Can you find the command that quits the game and remove it to make the game easier to play?

△ Don't shoot!

Why not add another Actor to the game to distract the player in the hope they'll click on that object by mistake? For instance, a red ball might look similar enough to an apple to fool the player!

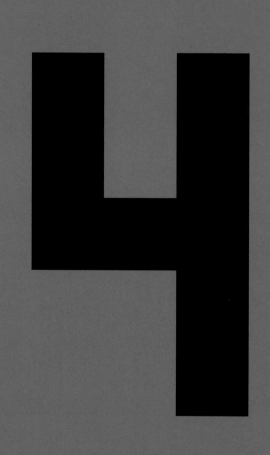

Coin Collector

How to build Coin Collector

Help a crafty fox collect as many coins as possible before the time runs out. The more coins you get, the higher your score. Be quick! You only have a few seconds to collect them.

What happens

A fox and a coin appear on the screen. You use the arrow keys to move the fox toward the coin. When the fox touches the coin, you get ten points, and another coin appears somewhere else. The game ends after seven seconds and the final score is displayed.

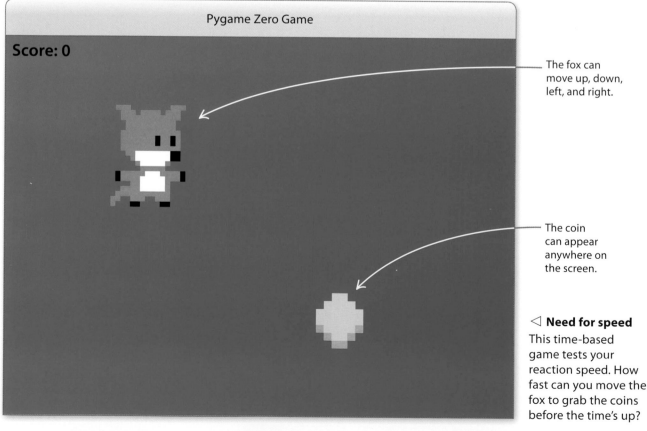

The fox can move up, down, left, and right.

The coin can appear anywhere on the screen.

◁ **Need for speed**
This time-based game tests your reaction speed. How fast can you move the fox to grab the coins before the time's up?

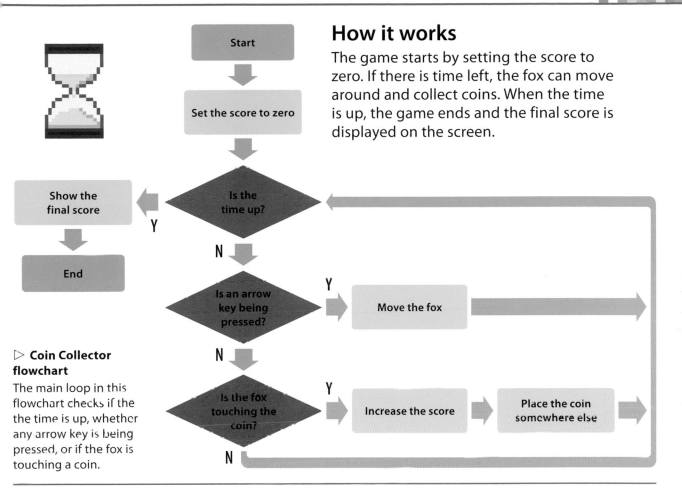

How it works

The game starts by setting the score to zero. If there is time left, the fox can move around and collect coins. When the time is up, the game ends and the final score is displayed on the screen.

▷ **Coin Collector flowchart**

The main loop in this flowchart checks if the the time is up, whether any arrow key is being pressed, or if the fox is touching a coin.

Getting started

Follow these steps to build the game. First set up a new file and import the relevant modules. Then draw the Actors and define the functions to run the game. Good luck!

Get set up
Create a new folder called *coin-collector*. Then open IDLE and create an empty file by going to the **File** menu and choosing **New File**. Select **Save As...** from the same menu and save the file as *coin.py* in the coin-collector folder.

2 **Set up an image folder**

This game uses two images—a fox and a coin. Within your coin-collector folder, create a new folder called *images*. Remember, this new folder needs to be in the same place as your coin.py file.

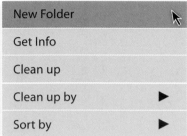

3 **Put the images into the folder**

Find the files called "coin.png" and "fox.png" in the Python Games Resource Pack (**dk.com/computercoding**). Copy them both into the images folder. Your folders should look like this now.

4 **Get coding**

Now you're ready to start coding. This game works in a similar way as Shoot the Fruit, so you'll be able to reuse some of the code from that game. Begin by setting the size of the playing area. Type this code at the top of your file.

```
WIDTH = 400
HEIGHT = 400
```

This code will make the game screen 400 pixels tall and 400 pixels wide.

5 **Setting the score**

Now, let's set the score to zero to begin with. You'll need to use a variable to do this. Type the code shown in black below.

```
WIDTH = 400
HEIGHT = 400
score = 0
```

This sets up a variable called **score**.

 LINGO

Patterns

Lots of computer games follow patterns. Even though two games might have different characters, power-ups, or levels, their actual rules may be quite similar. Computer programmers often look for patterns in the programs they are building. If they spot a pattern, they can reuse some code from an existing program, making it easier and quicker to build the new program. This code is also less likely to have bugs because it will already have been tested.

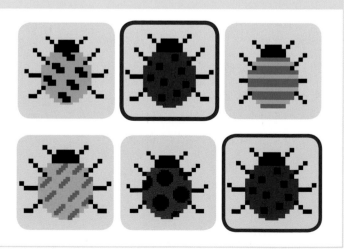

6 Game over?

You also need a Boolean variable (a variable whose value can either be True or False) to tell Pygame Zero if the game is over or not. At this stage, set the variable to False.

```
WIDTH = 400
HEIGHT = 400
score = 0
game_over = False
```

7 Introducing the Actors

This game will feature two Actors—a fox and a coin. To create them and set their positions, add these lines of code under what you typed in Step 6.

```
fox = Actor("fox")
fox.pos = 100, 100

coin = Actor("coin")
coin.pos = 200, 200
```

This line uses the fox.png file in the images folder to create the fox Actor.

The coin is positioned 200 pixels along from the top left and 200 pixels down.

8 Time to draw

Now you need to use the **draw()** function to display the Actors on the screen, change the background color, and display the score. Type in this code to do these.

These lines draw the fox and coin on the screen.

```
coin.pos = 200, 200

def draw():
    screen.fill("green")
    fox.draw()
    coin.draw()
    screen.draw.text("Score: " + str(score), color="black", topleft=(10, 10))
```

This line will display the score in the top-left corner of the screen.

9 Try it out

Now test the code you've written so far. Remember, you have to use the command line in the Command Prompt or Terminal window to do this.

`pgzrun` Drag the coin.py file here to run it.

Pages 24–25 will help you run the code if you've forgotten how.

10 Did it work?

Did your game run? You should see the fox and coin on your screen, with the score in the top-left corner. You can't actually play the game yet, but it's a good idea to run your code frequently to check for bugs.

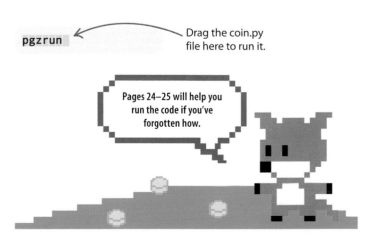

11 Using placeholders

You need to write some more functions in order to finish the game. You can add function placeholders without having to define them right away by using the keyword **pass**. Type in this code to give yourself a template of the functions you'll need.

The next question is... What is a function?
?

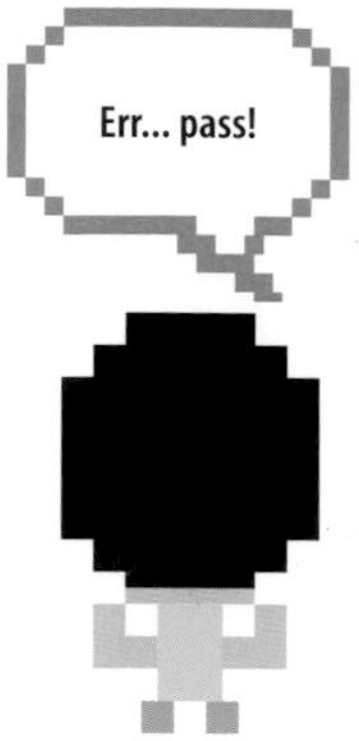
Err... pass!

```
    coin.draw()
    screen.draw.text("Score: " + str(score), color="black", topleft=(10, 10))

def place_coin():
    pass

def time_up():
    pass

def update():
    pass
```

To get an idea of the code's structure, you can use placeholders for functions that you'll finish coding later.

12 Importing randint()

Now it's time to define these functions. The first one will use Python's built-in **randint()** function, so you need to import it into your program. Type this line at the very top of your code to import it.

```
from random import randint
```

Make sure you type this before all the code you've written so far.

13 Placing the coin

Next change the code in your **place_coin()** function. This function will place the coin in a random position on the screen. Delete **pass** and type in these commands.

```
def place_coin():
    coin.x = randint(20, (WIDTH - 20))
    coin.y = randint(20, (HEIGHT - 20))
```

The coin will be placed at least 20 pixels in from the sides of the screen.

14 Run the function

Remember, it's not enough just to define the function; you have to run it, too. Add this line of code to the very bottom of your game.

```
def update():
    pass

place_coin()
```

This will run the code you've saved in the **place_coin()** function.

EXPERT TIPS

Pass

In Python, if you're not sure what code you want inside a function yet, you can use the **pass** keyword in its place, and then come back to it later. It's a bit like skipping a question in a quiz but answering it later.

15 Time's up!
Now let's fill in the code for the **time_up()** function. In this function, set the **game_over** Boolean variable to True, which will tell the program to quit the game when the function is called. Type in the following code.

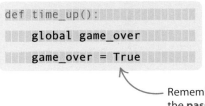

```
def time_up():
    global game_over
    game_over = True
```

↖ Remember to delete the **pass** keyword and then add these lines.

16 Set the timer
Now that **time_up()** is defined, the program needs to run it. But it needs to run seven seconds after the game starts. You can use Pygame Zero's built-in tool **clock** to do this. This tool lets the program call a function after a specified amount of time. Add this line in the code as shown here.

```
clock.schedule(time_up, 7.0)
place_coin()
```

↖ This line will run the function **time_up()** seven seconds after the game starts.

17 Ending the game
The game starts and then seven seconds later, **clock.schedule** will run the **time_up()** function, which ends the game. But the game still needs to show the player's final score. For this, you need to add in one more bit of code to the **draw()** function.

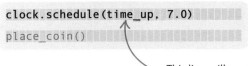

Time's up! I think you better stop now.

```
def draw():
    screen.fill("green")
    fox.draw()
    coin.draw()
    screen.draw.text("Score: " + str(score), color="black", topleft=(10, 10))

    if game_over:
        screen.fill("pink")
        screen.draw.text("Final Score: " + str(score), topleft=(10, 10), fontsize=60)
```

↖ If the variable **game_over** is True, this will turn the screen pink.

↗ The final score is shown on the screen.

↗ This command sets the size of the text shown on the screen.

18 Using update()
The final function you need to define is **update()**. This is a built-in Pygame Zero function, which means that unlike the other functions, you don't need to worry about when to run it. Once you've defined it, Pygame Zero will run it automatically—60 times a second! Delete **pass** under **def update()** and add this code. It will move the fox to the left if the left keyboard arrow is pressed.

```
def update():
    if keyboard.left:
        fox.x = fox.x - 2
```

↗ This moves the fox two pixels to the left if the left arrow is pressed.

19 **One way only**

Now test your code. You should be able to move the fox to the left. But the fox needs to be able to move in other directions, too, so add this code to do that.

```
def update():
    if keyboard.left:
        fox.x = fox.x - 2
    elif keyboard.right:
        fox.x = fox.x + 2
    elif keyboard.up:
        fox.y = fox.y - 2
    elif keyboard.down:
        fox.y = fox.y + 2
```

The else-if branches are used to move the fox depending on which arrow key is pressed.

20 **Collect the coins**

Finally, you need to add some code that will update the score if the fox touches a coin. Add this code to the **update()** function.

Make sure you add this line at the very top.

If the fox touches the coin, this variable will be True.

```
def update():
    global score

    if keyboard.left:
        fox.x = fox.x - 2
    elif keyboard.right:
        fox.x = fox.x + 2
    elif keyboard.up:
        fox.y = fox.y - 2
    elif keyboard.down:
        fox.y = fox.y + 2

    coin_collected = fox.colliderect(coin)

    if coin_collected:
        score = score + 10
        place_coin()

clock.schedule(time_up, 7.0)
place_coin()
```

21 **Game complete!**

You've written all the code, and your game is now ready to go! Test your game and see how many coins you can collect before the game is over.

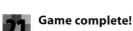

Look what I found!

This will increase the score by ten.

Hacks and tweaks

There are lots of ways to modify your game. You could try changing the fox to a different character of your choice, or you could make the game last longer.

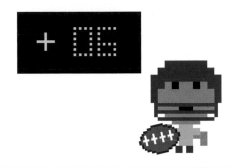

```
clock.schedule(time_up, 15.0)
```

△ Extra time
The game currently ends after seven seconds. To make the game easier, you could give the player more time to play. You can do this by changing just one line of code.

Name's Hog...
Hedge Hog.

```
hedgehog = Actor("hedgehog")
```

△ A different Actor
You can replace the fox with some other character by using another image from the Python Games Resource Pack, or you can use the 8-bit editors available online to make your own Actor. Remember to update the code so it uses the name of the new character throughout the program.

I think I can go faster.

```
if keyboard.left:
    fox.x = fox.x - 4
elif keyboard.right:
    fox.x = fox.x + 4
elif keyboard.up:
    fox.y = fox.y - 4
elif keyboard.down:
    fox.y = fox.y + 4
```

△ Go faster!
You can tweak the code to make the fox move faster. For this, you'll need to change some of the code in the **update()** function. At the moment, the fox moves two pixels every time the arrows are pressed. Here's a way to make it move at double that speed.

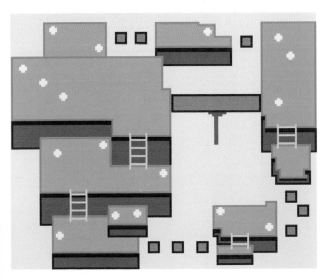

△ Change the playing area
You can change the size of the playing area by changing the values of **WIDTH** and **HEIGHT**. Try using different numbers for these values and see what happens. Can you spot which part of the code you need to update?

Follow the Numbers

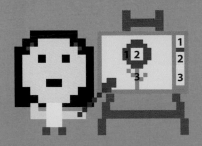

How to build Follow the Numbers

Can you connect all the dots in the correct order? Challenge yourself to finish the game as quickly as you can. Be careful, however—one wrong click and you'll have to start all over again.

What happens

At the beginning of the game, ten dots appear at random positions on the screen, each with a number next to it. You need to click on the dots in the correct order to connect them. The game will finish once you've connected all the dots together. But if you make a mistake, all the lines will disappear and you'll have to start from the very first dot again.

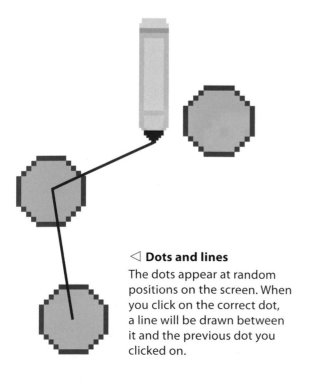

◁ **Dots and lines**
The dots appear at random positions on the screen. When you click on the correct dot, a line will be drawn between it and the previous dot you clicked on.

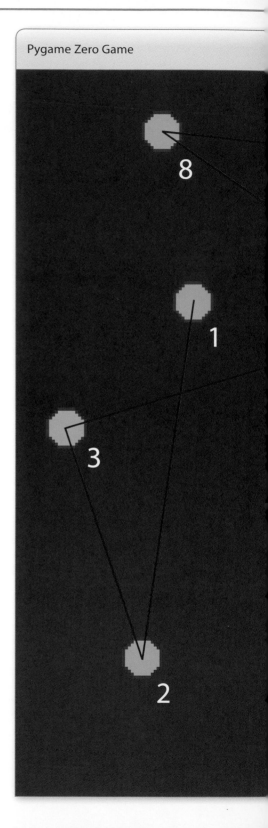

Pygame Zero Game

8

1

3

2

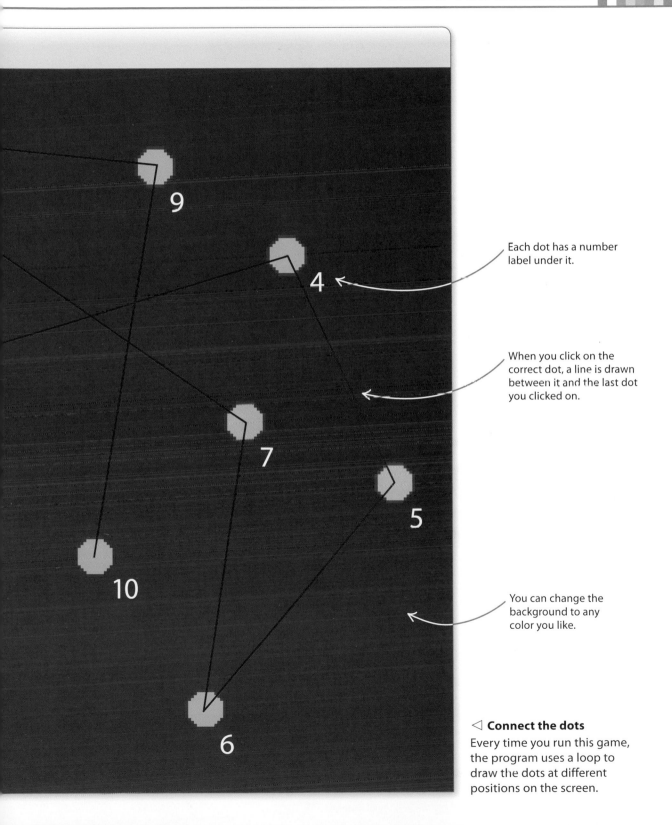

Each dot has a number label under it.

When you click on the correct dot, a line is drawn between it and the last dot you clicked on.

You can change the background to any color you like.

◁ **Connect the dots**
Every time you run this game, the program uses a loop to draw the dots at different positions on the screen.

How it works

This game uses Python's **randint()** function to randomly choose x and y coordinates for each of the dots, and then places them all on the screen. It uses the **on_mouse_down()** function to know when the player has clicked on a dot. If the player clicks on the correct dot, and it's not the first dot, a line is drawn between the current dot and the previous dot. If the player clicks on the wrong dot, or clicks anywhere else on the screen, all the lines are deleted and the player has to start again. The game ends once the player has connected all the dots.

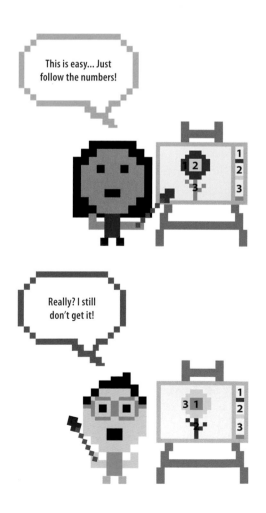

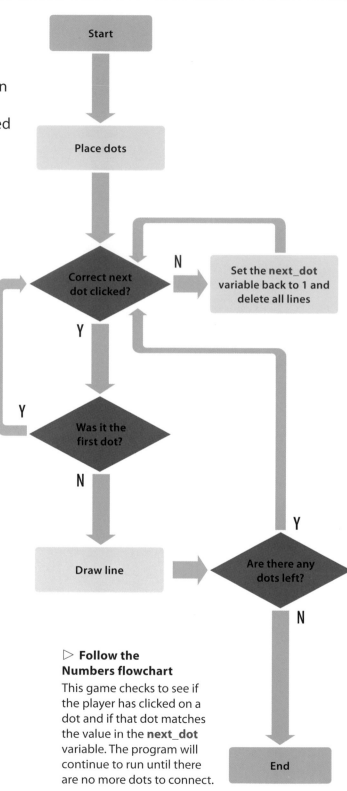

▷ **Follow the Numbers flowchart**

This game checks to see if the player has clicked on a dot and if that dot matches the value in the **next_dot** variable. The program will continue to run until there are no more dots to connect.

Let's get started

It's time to start building the game. Begin by importing the Python modules required for this game. Then write the functions to create the dots and the lines.

1 Set it up
Open IDLE and create an empty file by going to the **File** menu and choosing **New File**.

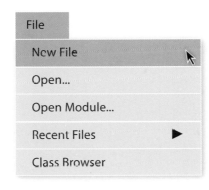

One piece at a time!

2 Save the game
Go to the python-games folder you made earlier and create another folder in it called *follow-the-numbers*. Go to the **File** menu, click **Save As...** and save your program as *numbers.py*.

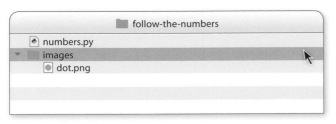

Save As:	numbers.py
Tags:	
Where:	follow-the-numbers

Cancel   Save

3 Set up an image folder
This game uses one image for all the dots. Create a new folder called *images* inside your follow-the-numbers folder.

New Folder
Get Info
Clean up
Clean up by ▶
Sort by ▶

4 Put the image into the folder
Find the file called "dot.png" in the Python Games Resource Pack (**dk.com/computercoding**) and copy it into the images folder. Your folders should look something like this now.

follow-the-numbers
- numbers.py
- images
  - dot.png

5 Import a module
Now you're ready to start coding. Go back to your IDLE file and type this line at the top.

```
from random import randint
```

This imports the **randint()** function from Python's Random module.

6 Set the screen size

Next you need to set the size of the screen for your game. Type these lines under the code from Step 5.

```
WIDTH = 400
HEIGHT = 400
```

This declares the global variables to set the screen size in pixels.

I definitely need a bigger screen!

7 Set up the lists

Now you need some lists to store all the dots, and also the lines that will be drawn to connect these dots. You'll need a variable to keep track of which dot should be clicked on next. Create these by typing this code.

```
HEIGHT = 400


dots = []

lines = []


next_dot = 0
```

These global lists will store the dots and the lines.

This global variable starts at **0** and tells the game which dot should be clicked on next.

You need to stand on the mark, Martha.

8 Set up the Actors

It's time to set up the Actors. In this game, the ten dots are the Actors. Create these dots in a loop, giving each one a randomly chosen position and then adding it to the list of Actors. Type this code under what you typed in Step 7.

This line will create a new Actor using the image of the dot in the images folder.

This will ensure that the dots appear at least 20 pixels away from the edge of the screen so the whole dot is shown.

```
next_dot = 0


for dot in range(0, 10):
    actor = Actor("dot")
    actor.pos = randint(20, WIDTH - 20), \
    randint(20, HEIGHT - 20)
    dots.append(actor)
```

This will loop ten times.

Use a backslash character if you need to split a long line of code over two lines. It may fit on one in your file, though.

9 Draw the Actors

Now use the **draw()** function to display the dots and their number labels on the screen. The function **screen.draw.text()** expects a string as an input, but since the value stored in **number** is an integer, you need to use the **str()** function to convert it into a string. Add this code below the commands from Step 8.

This sets the background color to black.

```
dots.append(actor)

def draw():
    screen.fill("black")
    number = 1
    for dot in dots:
        screen.draw.text(str(number), \
                        (dot.pos[0], dot.pos[1] + 12))
        dot.draw()
        number = number + 1
```

This creates a variable to keep track of the current number label.

These lines draw each dot on the screen along with a number label.

10 Draw the lines

Next add this code to the end of the **draw()** function to draw the lines. Until the player clicks on the first two dots, the lines list will remain empty, so the function won't draw any lines on the screen.

```
        number = number + 1
    for line in lines:
        screen.draw.line(line[0], line[1], (100, 0, 0))
```

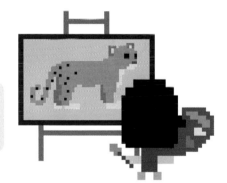

 EXPERT TIPS

Line function

This function draws a line between two points on the screen—starting at point x and ending at point y. You can change the color of the line to red (R), green (G), blue (B), or even a mix of all three (RGB). Create a color by assigning values between 0 (none of the color) and 255 (the maximum amount of the color). For example, (0, 0, 100) sets the color of the line to blue. You can use some colors by typing in their names, but RGB values let you use lots of different shades.

```
screen.draw.line(x, y, (0, 0, 100))
```

These numbers can change depending on the color you choose for the line.

How about royal blue? Or pink? Better check pages 114–115 for their RGB values.

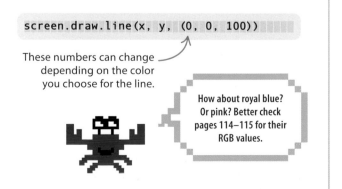

Hacks and tweaks

Try out the following ideas to make Follow the Numbers a bit more challenging and even more fun.

Strike three, and you're out!

△ **No more chances**

At the moment, the player has an unlimited number of attempts to connect the dots together. Try changing the code so that the game ends if the player makes a mistake. You could even add a "Game Over!" message to your code. If you do this, remember to clear everything else off the screen first.

△ **More dots**

You can add more dots to the game to make it more challenging. Remember the loop in Step 8 that creates ten dots? Can you modify the range to create some more?

Set up a variable to keep track of how many dots each level has.

Define a function that adds two dots to the **dots** list.

```
number_of_dots = 10


def next_level:


if next_dot == number_of_dots - 1:
```

What does your program need to do when increasing the level?

△ **Level up**

You could add levels so the game gets harder each time you complete a sequence. Each level could have two more dots than the last. Try defining a **next_level()** function to do this. This code will help you get started.

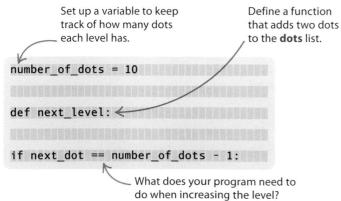

△ **Multiple sets of dots**

To make the game more challenging, you could add another set of dots. There's a red dot in the Hacks and tweaks section of the Resource Pack. You'll need to think about the following things to tweak the game:

- Create a separate list for the red dots.
- Create a separate list for blue lines to connect the red dots.
- Create a **next_dot** variable for the red dots.
- Set up the red dots at the start.
- Draw the red dots and blue lines.
- Check if the next red dot has been clicked.

I'm still going to win, you know. Get ready to lose again!

STAIRS

▷ **In record time**

You can use the system clock to time how long it takes a player to connect all the dots. You could then try to beat your friends' times! To time the game, you'll need to use the **time()** function. Once the game is complete, you can display the final time taken on the screen. Why not try placing the clock in the corner? Remember to use **str()** to cast the message into a string. You can check Step 9 of the game if you need to remind yourself how to do this. At the moment, though, the **draw()** function is only called when the player clicks the mouse, so the clock would only update after each mouse click. To fix this, add this code. This function is called 60 times a second. Each call also calls the **draw()** function, so the clock stays up to date.

```
from time import time
```

Put this code at the top of your program to use the Time module.

```
def update():
    pass
```

You don't need to replace **pass** with any actual code.

 EXPERT TIPS
time()

The **time()** function might give you an unexpected result. It calculates the time that's passed since an "epoch," which is the date an operating system considers to be the "start of time." Windows machines will tell you how many seconds have passed since January 1, 1601! You can use this simple calculation below to work out how long it actually took the player to complete the game.

```
total_time = end_time - start_time
```

This calculates the total time elapsed.

EXPERT TIPS
round()

The **time()** function calculates time to lots of decimal places. You can use the **round()** function to round it to a certain number of decimal places, which will make it easier to read. **round()** takes two parameters—the number to round up or down and the number of decimal places to shorten it to.

```
>>> round(5.75, 1)
5.8
```

This is the number of decimal places you want to round it to.

This is the number you want to round up.

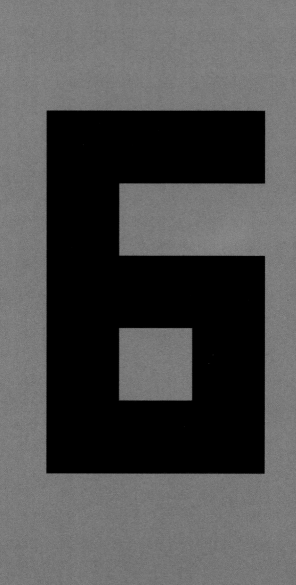

Red Alert

How to build Red Alert

You'll need lightning-fast reactions to beat this game. Click on the red star to keep the game moving. Anything other than red will land you in trouble.

What happens

When the game begins, two stars appear and start moving down the screen. The player needs to click on the red star before the stars reach the bottom of the screen. Each time the red star is clicked, the game moves on to the next level. With each level, more green and blue stars are added and they move faster than before. If the player clicks on any star other than the red one, or if the stars reach the bottom of the screen, the game ends.

The number of stars increases with every level.

◁ **Stars**
This game uses three colors for the star Actors—red, blue, and green.

Pygame Zero Game

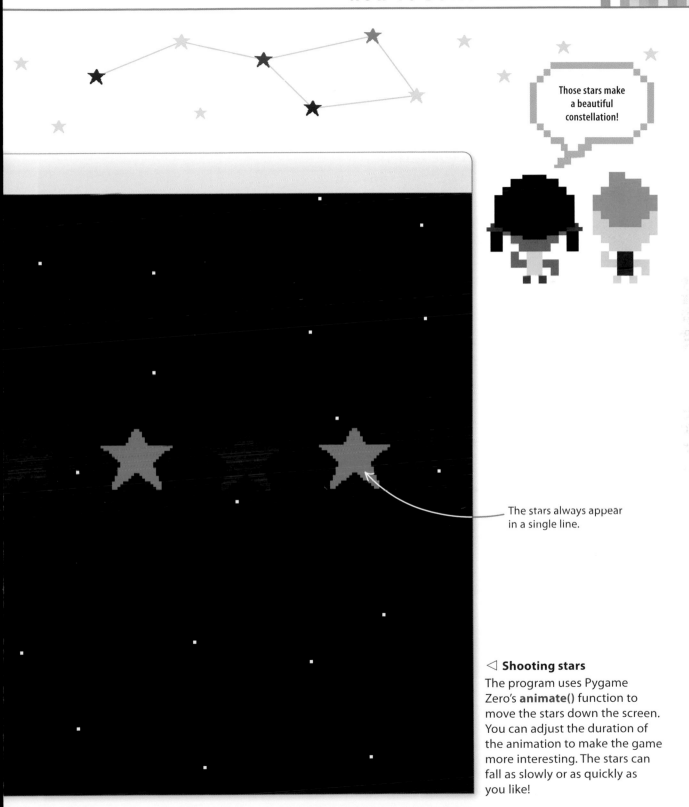

Those stars make a beautiful constellation!

The stars always appear in a single line.

◁ **Shooting stars**
The program uses Pygame Zero's **animate()** function to move the stars down the screen. You can adjust the duration of the animation to make the game more interesting. The stars can fall as slowly or as quickly as you like!

How it works

This game uses the **draw()** and **update()** functions to display the stars on the screen. Each time the **draw()** function is called, the program clears everything on the screen and redraws the stars. The **update()** function checks if the player has clicked on a star.

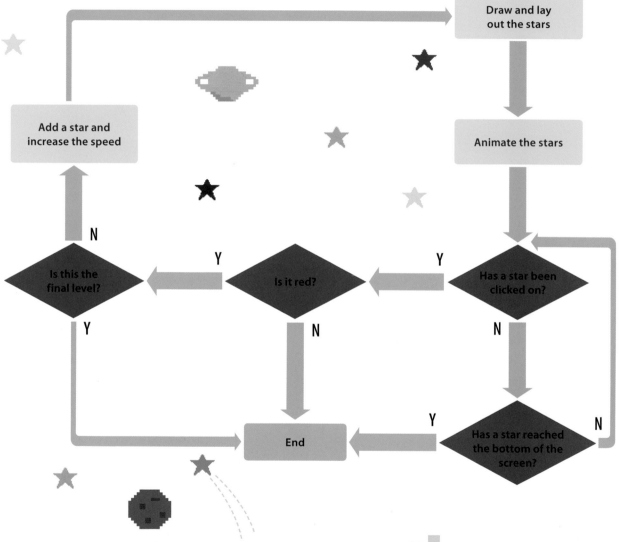

△ **Red Alert flowchart**

This program uses one main loop that checks if the stars are moving down the screen and if the player has clicked on a star. The game either ends or moves on to the next level, depending on the player's action.

Let's begin

It's time to start coding the game. First you'll add the variables that control the game's behavior. Then you'll create the functions that draw and move the stars. Once the steps are complete, you should have some colorful stars.

Ouch! I'm seeing stars!

1 Create a new file
To get started, open IDLE and create an empty file by going to the **File** menu and choosing **New File**.

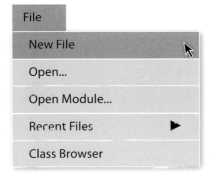

File
New File
Open...
Open Module...
Recent Files ▶
Class Browser

2 Save the file
Go to the python-games folder you made earlier. Inside this folder, create another folder called *red-alert* and save your IDLE file in it as *red.py*.

Save As:	red.py
Tags:	
Where:	red-alert

Cancel Save

3 Set up an image folder
This game uses images of a red star, a blue star, and a green star. Create a new folder, called *images*, inside the red-alert folder to save these images. It should be in the same place as the red.py file.

New Folder
Get Info
Clean up
Clean up by ▶
Sort by ▶

4 Put the images in the folder
Find the Red Alert images in the Python Games Resource Pack (**dk.com/computercoding**) and copy them into the images folder you just created. Your folders should look something like this now.

red-alert
red.py
▼ images
★ blue-star.png
★ green-star.png
★ red-star.png
space.png

5 Import a module

The first thing you need to do is import Python's Random module. To import a whole module, you simply need to type **import** followed by the name of the module. We'll use Random in the **choice()** and **shuffle()** functions later in the code.

```
import random
```

This imports the Random module.

This sets the font color of the message that is displayed at the end of the game.

6 Declare the constants

Constants are variables that are usually declared at the start of a program. They are called constants because their values shouldn't change throughout the program. Type the code shown in black.

```
import random

FONT_COLOR = (255, 255, 255)
WIDTH = 800
HEIGHT = 600
CENTER_X = WIDTH / 2
CENTER_Y = HEIGHT / 2
CENTER = (CENTER_X, CENTER_Y)
FINAL_LEVEL = 6
START_SPEED = 10
COLORS = ["green", "blue"]
```

These constants define the size of the game window.

This constant defines the number of levels in the game.

This sets the speed at which the stars move down the screen.

This line sets the color of the stars that should not be clicked.

7 Declare the global variables

Like constants, global variables are usually declared at the top of a program, but unlike constants, their values can change throughout the program. They can be used throughout the code. In this game, you'll use these global variables to track the game's progress. Add this code under the lines from Step 6.

```
FINAL_LEVEL = 6
START_SPEED = 10
COLORS = ["green", "blue"]

game_over = False
game_complete = False
current_level = 1
stars = []
animations = []
```

These variables will keep track of if the game is over or not.

This variable will keep track of what level the player's on.

These lists will keep track of the stars on the screen.

▪▪▪ LINGO

Constants

Constants are variables whose value shouldn't change after they are first set. Programmers use capital letters when naming them to let other programmers know not to change their values. This is known as a "naming convention"—a rule that most programmers agree on, so that everyone's code looks similar and is easier to understand.

8 **Draw the stars**

Now it's time to define the first function. You'll use the **draw()** function to add some stars and display messages on the screen. Add this code under what you typed in Step 7.

```
current_level = 1
stars = []
animations = []


def draw():
    global stars, current_level, game_over, game_complete
    screen.clear()
    screen.blit("space", (0, 0))
    if game_over:
        display_message("GAME OVER!", "Try again.")
    elif game_complete:
        display_message("YOU WON!", "Well done.")
    else:
        for star in stars:
            star.draw()
```

These are the global variables used in this function.

This adds a background image to the game window.

When the game is over or complete, this block displays the relevant message on the screen.

This block draws the stars on the screen.

9 **Define the update() function**
The **draw()** function that you defined in the previous step will have nothing to draw unless you create the stars. Define the **update()** function next to check if there are any stars in the **stars** list. If there aren't, it should call the **make_stars()** function. Add this code under the lines from Step 8.

```
            star.draw()

def update():
    global stars
    if len(stars) == 0:
        stars = make_stars(current_level)
```

This checks if any stars have been created yet.

If the **stars** list is empty, this function is called.

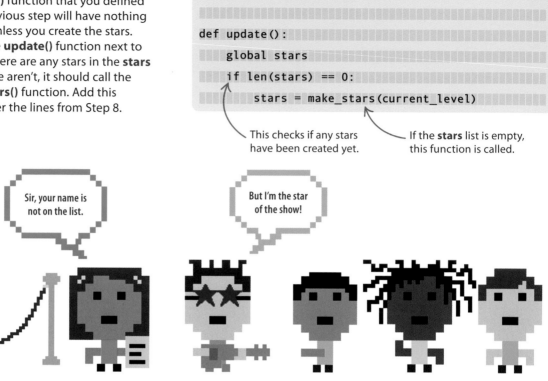

10 **Make the stars**
Next you need to define the **make_stars()** function. This is used to call some of the other functions in the game. Type this after the code from Step 9.

This returns a list of colors that will be used to draw the stars.

```
        stars = make_stars(current_level)

def make_stars(number_of_extra_stars):
    colors_to_create = get_colors_to_create(number_of_extra_stars)
    new_stars = create_stars(colors_to_create)
    layout_stars(new_stars)
    animate_stars(new_stars)
    return new_stars
```

This function uses the list of colors as a parameter and creates Actors for each star.

This function puts the stars in the right position on the screen.

This function makes the stars move down the screen.

Don't forget to save your work.

11 Add placeholders

You'll need to define all the functions created in the previous step before you can test the game. For now, use **return []** for the **get_colors_to_create()** and **create_stars()** functions to make empty lists, then write placeholders for the **layout_stars()** and **animate_stars()** functions by using the **pass** keyword. Add the code shown here.

```
    return new_stars


def get_colors_to_create(number_of_extra_stars):
    return []


def create_stars(colors_to_create):
    return []


def layout_stars(stars_to_layout):
    pass


def animate_stars(stars_to_animate):
    pass
```

12 Test the code

Save the IDLE file and run it from the command line in the Command Prompt or Terminal window. You won't see any stars on the screen yet, but you will be able to check if there are any bugs in the code.

```
pgzrun
```

Drag the red.py file here to run it.

13 Get a list of colors

This game uses red, blue, and green stars. First create a list containing a string for the color red and then assign this list to the variable **colors_to_create**. The list starts with red, because you always need one—and only one—red star to appear. To add green and blue stars, you'll use the parameter **number_of_extra_stars** to loop through the code, randomly adding either green or blue to the list of colors. Replace **return []** under **def get_colors_to_create(number_of_extra_stars)** from Step 11 with this code.

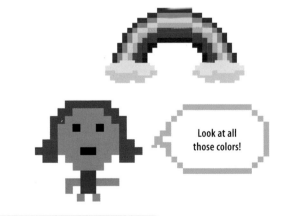

Look at all those colors!

```
def get_colors_to_create(number_of_extra_stars):
    colors_to_create = ["red"]
    for i in range(0, number_of_extra_stars):
        random_color = random.choice(COLORS)
        colors_to_create.append(random_color)
    return colors_to_create
```

This makes the first star in the list red.

i refers to the current number in the range.

This chooses a random color from the list for each additional star.

This adds the new color to the list.

14 Create the stars

Now you need to create the stars on the screen. Start by making an empty list called **new_stars**. Then loop over the colors in the **colors_to_create** list. With each loop, the code will create a new star Actor for the current color and add it to the **new_stars** list. Replace **return []** under **def create_stars(colors_to_create)** with the code shown in black.

This list will store the new stars that are created.

This loops over the **colors_to_create** list.

```
def create_stars(colors_to_create):
    new_stars = []
    for color in colors_to_create:
        star = Actor(color + "-star")
        new_stars.append(star)
    return new_stars
```

This returns the updated **new_stars** list.

This combines the two strings.

Do you think that's enough stars, or should I create some more?

15 Try it out

Check your code to make sure no bugs have crawled in. Save your code and run it from the command line. What do you see on the screen?

At this point, both of the stars will be drawn on top of each other in the top-left corner.

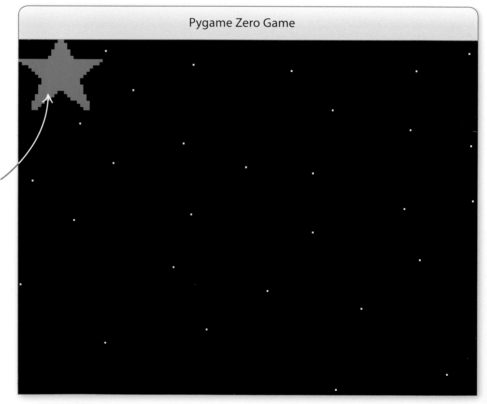

Pygame Zero Game

Place the stars

In this step, you'll use the **layout_stars()** function to place all the stars in the right position. First you need to work out the number of gaps you need between the stars. This number will be one more than the number of stars on the screen. For example, if there are two stars on the screen, there will be three gaps. The size of each gap can be worked out by dividing the width of the screen by the total number of gaps. You also need to shuffle the position of the stars so that the red star doesn't appear at the same position every time. Replace **pass** under **def layout_stars(stars_to_layout)** with the code below.

This calculates the number of gaps on the screen.

This divides the width of the screen by the number of gaps.

This shuffles the position of the stars along the x-axis.

```
def layout_stars(stars_to_layout):
    number_of_gaps = len(stars_to_layout) + 1
    gap_size = WIDTH / number_of_gaps
    random.shuffle(stars_to_layout)
    for index, star in enumerate(stars_to_layout):
        new_x_pos = (index + 1) * gap_size
        star.x = new_x_pos
```

This block sets the position of the current star along the x-axis by multiplying the position of the star in the list by the size of the gap.

Test again

Run the program one more time to see what's changed in the code.

The gap between the edge of the screen and each star is the same size as the gap between the two stars. This gap is represented by the yellow dotted line here.

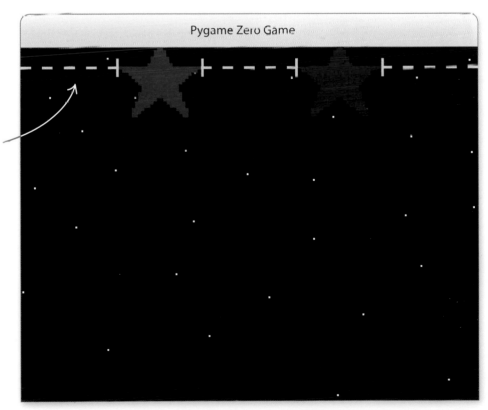

18 **Animate the stars**

Now that you have a few stars on the screen, it's time to add animation and bring this game to life. You need to write some code to move each star down the screen. You'll also have to define the duration of the animation so the stars move faster as the levels progress. You'll set the star's anchor to the bottom so that the animation stops as soon as the star reaches the bottom of the screen. Replace **pass** under **def animate_stars(stars_to_animate)** from Step 11 with the code below.

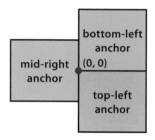

LINGO

Anchor

In computer graphics, "anchor" refers to a point on a shape. This point is used to determine the shape's position on the screen. For example, if the anchor of a square is the bottom-left corner, when you set the position of the square to (0, 0), its bottom-left corner is placed exactly at the (0, 0) coordinates.

This works out the duration of the animation by subtracting the current level from the default start speed of the star. The higher the level, the shorter the duration, so the faster the animation.

```
def animate_stars(stars_to_animate):
    for star in stars_to_animate:
        duration = START_SPEED - current_level
        star.anchor = ("center", "bottom")
        animation = animate(star, duration=duration, on_finished=handle_game_over, y=HEIGHT)
        animations.append(animation)
```

This sets the star's anchor at the bottom of the star image.

This calls the **handle_game_over()** function when the animation is complete.

19 **Game over**

Next you need to define the **handle_game_over()** function, which will end the game if the player makes a mistake. Type the code shown in black after the code from Step 18.

```
        animations.append(animation)


def handle_game_over():
    global game_over
    game_over = True
```

Game over? It can't be true!

GAME OVER!

EXPERT TIPS

Animate function

animate() is a very useful function in Pygame Zero's library. It makes it really easy to move an Actor on the screen. This function takes a number of parameters:

- The first parameter is always the Actor that you want to animate.
- **tween=** This optional parameter can be used to change the behavior of the animation.
- **duration=** This parameter is the number of seconds the animation lasts for.

- **on_finished=** This is an optional parameter that allows you to pass a function that you want to call once the animation is finished. In Red Alert, you use this parameter to end the game when the star reaches the bottom of the screen.
- The final parameters are the properties of the Actor you want to animate. There can be more than one property. For example, if the Actor is at (0, 0) coordinates and you want to move it to (100, 0), the **animate()** function will move the Actor to the right by 100 pixels. This move will be smooth and will last as many seconds as you set the **duration** parameter.

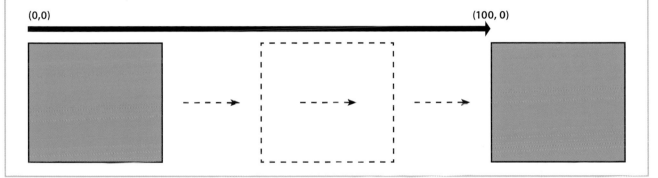

20 **Handle mouse clicks**

It's time to create a function that allows the player to interact with the game. Use Pygame Zero's **on_mouse_down()** function to do this. This function is called whenever the player clicks the mouse. Then use the **collidepoint()** function to check if the player has clicked on a star. If they have, the code will check whether that star was red or not. Type this code under the lines from Step 19.

```
game_over = True

def on_mouse_down(pos):
    global stars, current_level
    for star in stars:
        if star.collidepoint(pos):  ◀
            if "red" in star.image:
                red_star_click()
            else:
                handle_game_over()
```

This function is called if the player clicks on a red star.

This function is called if the player clicks on a star that is not red.

This checks if the player has clicked on a star.

21 Click a red star

In this game, when the player clicks on a red star, the program stops the animation of the current set of stars on the screen and moves the game to the next level. If the player is on the final level, **game_complete** is set to True and the game ends. Add this code after the lines from Step 20.

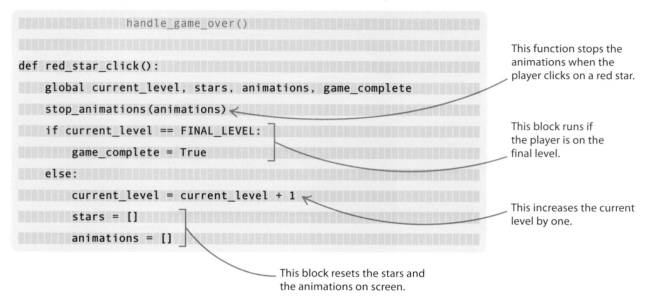

```
            handle_game_over()


def red_star_click():
    global current_level, stars, animations, game_complete
    stop_animations(animations)
    if current_level == FINAL_LEVEL:
        game_complete = True
    else:
        current_level = current_level + 1
        stars = []
        animations = []
```

This function stops the animations when the player clicks on a red star.

This block runs if the player is on the final level.

This increases the current level by one.

This block resets the stars and the animations on screen.

22 Stop the animations

Now you need to define the **stop_animations()** function. This function stops the stars from moving by looping over the list and calling **stop()** on each animation if it is currently running.

```
        animations = []


def stop_animations(animations_to_stop):
    for animation in animations_to_stop:
        if animation.running:
            animation.stop()
```

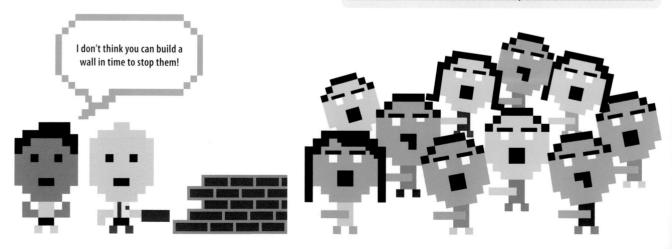

I don't think you can build a wall in time to stop them!

23 Display messages

Finally, add some code that displays the message you wrote in Step 8 when the game comes to an end. Add these lines under the code from Step 22.

```
                animation.stop()


def display_message(heading_text, sub_heading_text):
    screen.draw.text(heading_text, fontsize=60, center=CENTER, color=FONT_COLOR)
    screen.draw.text(sub_heading_text,
                     fontsize=30,
                     center=(CENTER_X, CENTER_Y + 30),
                     color=FONT_COLOR)
```

These display the text on the screen when the game ends.

This is the position of the second line of the message.

24 Time to play!

That's it! Save your program and run the IDLE file from the command line to start playing. How many levels can you complete?

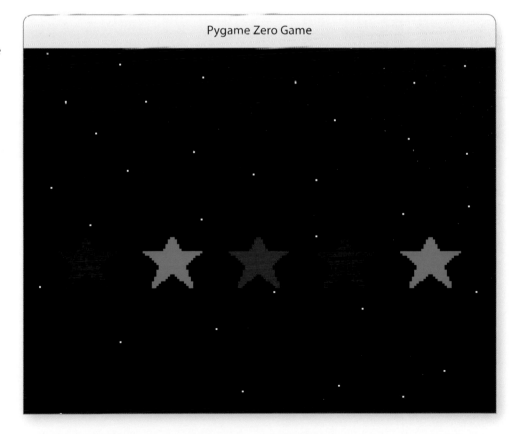

Pygame Zero Game

Hacks and tweaks

This is your chance to put your own stamp on the game.
We've suggested some changes you might want to try.
Give them a try and maybe combine them with your own
ideas to make something new and different.

> Bharti wait!
> I can change.

◁ **Change the Actor**

You can change the way your game
looks by simply changing the star Actor.
Find another image of an Actor in the
Python Games Resource Pack, or create
your own by using an 8-bit editor online.
Don't forget to update the name of
the Actor in the code.

▽ **A need for speed**

One way to make the game more challenging is to
make the stars move at different speeds. Add the code
given below to the **animate_stars()** function. It uses
the **randint()** function to set the speed to 0, 1, or 2.
Once you have a value to adjust the speed by, it can be
added to the animation duration. Try running the
game after adding this code.

```
random_speed_adjustment = random.randint(0,2)
duration = START_SPEED - current_level + random_speed_adjustment
```

```
        star.x = new_x_pos
    if index % 2 == 0:
            star.y = 0
    else:
            star.y = HEIGHT
```

◁ **Two directions**

If you want to keep the players on their toes, you can make the
stars appear from the opposite direction. First you'll need to
add the code shown here to the **layout stars()** function. This will
check if the current index number is odd or even. When it's odd,
the stars will appear at the bottom. Next you'll need to update the
animate_stars() function to make the stars move from the bottom
to the top. Remember to update the star's anchor.

I'm late for school! I'll try again tomorrow.

```
def update():
    global stars, game_complete, game_over, current_level
    if len(stars) == 0:
        stars = make_stars(current_level)
    if (game_complete or game_over) and keyboard.space:
        stars = []
        current_level = 1
        game_complete = False
        game_over = False
```

◁ **Try again**

At the moment, the player needs to quit the game to try again. You can add some code to allow the player to play again by pressing a key. Add some code to the **update()** function that will check if the player has pressed the **Space bar** when the game is over or complete. If they have, the game is reset. You'll also need to update the **draw()** function to change the message that is displayed at the end.

▽ **Shuffling**

You can make the game a bit more fun by adding some code that shuffles the stars every second. For this, you'll need to use the **shuffle()** function. This function first checks that the **stars** list isn't empty. It then uses a Python feature called list comprehension. This allows you to get each star's position along the x-axis in the form of a list. Once you have this list, you can mix up the values in it. Next you'll need to loop over the **stars** list and create an animation for each star to move them to their new position. Use **clock.schedule_interval()** to run the **shuffle()** function once every second. Add the following code at the end of your IDLE file.

```
def shuffle():
    global stars
    if stars:
        x_values = [star.x for star in stars]
        random.shuffle(x_values)
        for index, star in enumerate(stars):
            new_x = x_values[index]
            animation = animate(star, duration=0.5, x=new_x)
            animations.append(animation)

clock.schedule_interval(shuffle, 1)
```

I like the shuffle mode!

Big Quiz

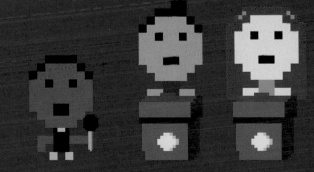

How to build Big Quiz

Put your coding skills to the test and create a quiz game to challenge your friends. You're the quizmaster, so you can make the questions about any topic you like.

What happens

When the game begins, the first question is shown on the screen along with four possible answers. The player has ten seconds to click on an answer box. If they get the right answer, the game moves on to the next question. If the player chooses a wrong answer, or if the time runs out, the game ends and the final score is displayed on the screen.

What is the capital of France?

Paris

△ **Boxes**
This game doesn't use images. Instead, the questions, answers, and the timer are displayed in colorful boxes that you create using code.

Each question is displayed here.

Pygame Zero Game

What is capital of

London

Berlin

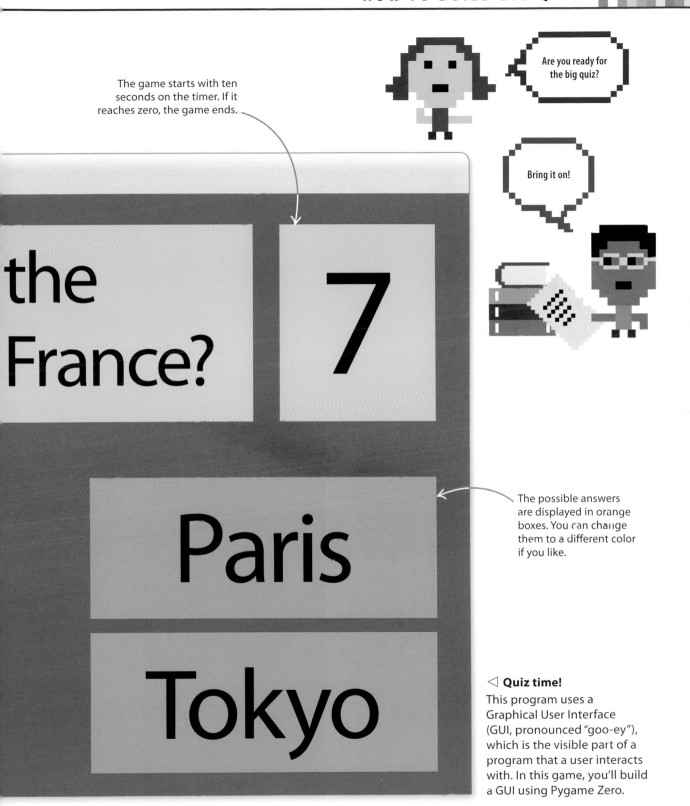

The game starts with ten seconds on the timer. If it reaches zero, the game ends.

the France?

7

Paris

Tokyo

Are you ready for the big quiz?

Bring it on!

The possible answers are displayed in orange boxes. You can change them to a different color if you like.

◁ **Quiz time!**
This program uses a Graphical User Interface (GUI, pronounced "goo-ey"), which is the visible part of a program that a user interacts with. In this game, you'll build a GUI using Pygame Zero.

How it works

All the questions and possible answers are stored in a list. The program uses the **pop()** function to get the first question and its possible answers from the list and then displays them. The player's score is stored in a variable and increases with each correct answer. The final score is displayed at the end of the game.

◁ **Big Quiz flowchart**
The main body of this program is a loop that checks if the player has selected the correct answer within the given time. If they have, the program moves to the next question in the list and the timer is reset. If the answer is wrong, the game ends and the final score is displayed.

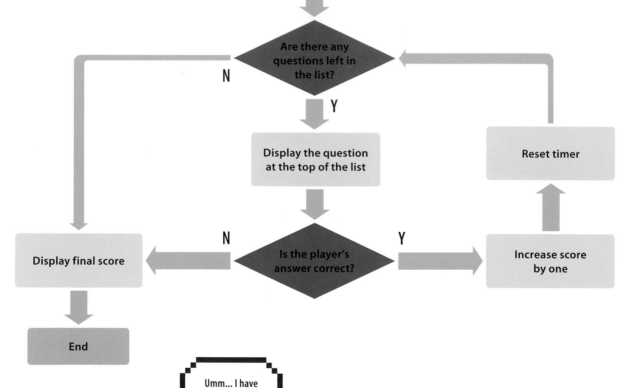

Thinking caps on!

There may be a time limit to answer the questions, but not to build the game! Follow these steps carefully to build your own quiz show to play with your friends and family.

1 **First steps**

Create a new folder called *big-quiz* in your python-games folder. Then open IDLE and create an empty file by going to the **File** menu and choosing **New File**. Select **Save As...** from the same menu and save the file as *quiz.py* in the big-quiz folder.

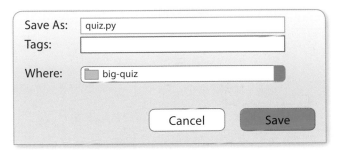

Save As:	quiz.py
Tags:	
Where:	📁 big-quiz

Cancel　　Save

2 **Set the screen size**

Next you need to define the size of the playing area. Add this code to the very top of your program to set the width and height of the game screen.

```
WIDTH = 1280
HEIGHT = 720
```
These values are in pixels.

3 **Create the stubs**

You don't need any images for this game, so you can jump straight into writing the code. First create placeholders for the functions you'll need to build the quiz.

Check page 144 to know more about placeholders.

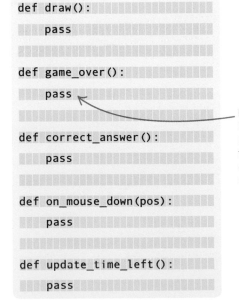
```
def draw():
    pass


def game_over():
    pass


def correct_answer():
    pass


def on_mouse_down(pos):
    pass


def update_time_left():
    pass
```

Remember, **pass** is used as a placeholder for functions that you don't want to define right away.

4 Plan the interface

When building this game, you need to think about the way it looks, or its "interface." The player needs to be able to see the question, its possible answers, and a timer that shows how long they've got left. Here's a sketch of how you might want the interface to look.

When planning the interface of a game, try sketching it on paper before writing any code.

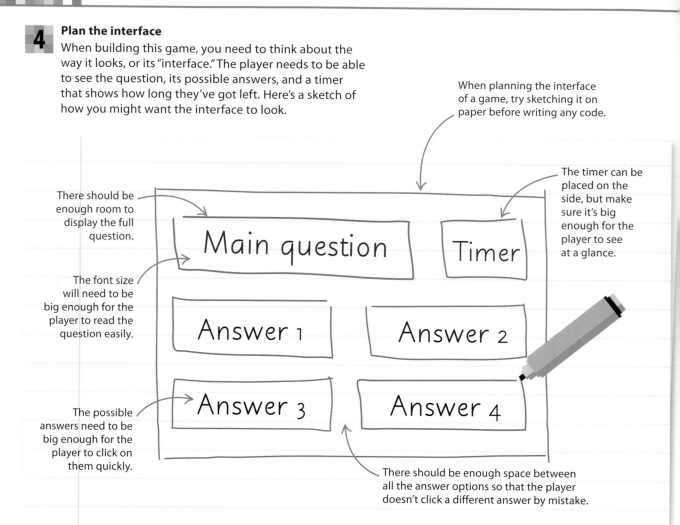

The timer can be placed on the side, but make sure it's big enough for the player to see at a glance.

There should be enough room to display the full question.

The font size will need to be big enough for the player to read the question easily.

The possible answers need to be big enough for the player to click on them quickly.

There should be enough space between all the answer options so that the player doesn't click a different answer by mistake.

Main question

Timer

Answer 1

Answer 2

Answer 3

Answer 4

. . . LINGO

Wireframes

Computer game designers can plan their game interfaces using wireframes. These are diagrams that show the different parts of an interface that the player sees on screen. They can be drawn by hand or made using a simple drawing tool on a computer. By doing this, the interface can be tested, and any changes to the design can be made before writing the code.

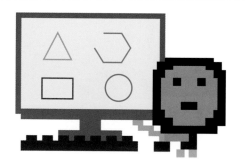

5 Create a box for the interface

Now that you've planned what the interface will look like, you can create the rectangular boxes that will make up the GUI. Type this code below what you typed in Step 2 to create a box for the main question.

```
WIDTH = 1280
HEIGHT = 720

main_box = Rect(0, 0, 820, 240)
```

This function takes four parameters. The first two numbers are the coordinates of the top-left corner of the box, and the last two numbers are the coordinates of the bottom-right corner of the box.

This sets the box size to 820 pixels wide and 240 pixels high.

6 Make the other boxes

You now need to make a box for the timer and four separate boxes for each of the possible answers. Type this code under what you wrote in Step 5.

```
main_box = Rect(0, 0, 820, 240)
timer_box = Rect(0, 0, 240, 240)
answer_box1 = Rect(0, 0, 495, 165)
answer_box2 = Rect(0, 0, 495, 165)
answer_box3 = Rect(0, 0, 495, 165)
answer_box4 = Rect(0, 0, 495, 165)
```

The timer box is a square 240 pixels wide and 240 pixels high.

All the answer boxes are the same size.

7 Move the boxes

At the moment, all the boxes will be drawn on top of each other in the top-left corner. You need to add some code to move them to their correct positions on the screen. Type this code immediately after the code from Step 6.

```
answer_box4 = Rect(0, 0, 495, 165)

main_box.move_ip(50, 40)
timer_box.move_ip(990, 40)
answer_box1.move_ip(50, 358)
answer_box2.move_ip(735, 358)
answer_box3.move_ip(50, 538)
answer_box4.move_ip(735, 538)
```

move_ip() moves each rectangle to the place you want it on the screen.

The top-left corner of each box will be placed at the coordinates in the brackets.

Arr! Time to move all these boxes into place!

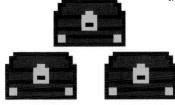

8 **Create a list of answer boxes**
This game uses four boxes to show the possible answers to each question. You can keep track of these boxes by using a list. Add this code immediately after what you typed in Step 7.

```
answer_box4.move_ip(735, 538)
answer_boxes = [answer_box1, answer_box2, answer_box3, answer_box4]
```

This list holds all the answer boxes.

9 **Draw the boxes**
Now that you've created the boxes, it's time to add some code to draw them on the screen. Replace **pass** under **def draw()** from Step 3 with this code.

This sets the background to a dim gray color.

These lines draw the main box and the timer on the screen and colors them sky blue.

```
def draw():
    screen.fill("dim gray")
    screen.draw.filled_rect(main_box, "sky blue")
    screen.draw.filled_rect(timer_box, "sky blue")

    for box in answer_boxes:
        screen.draw.filled_rect(box, "orange")
```

This draws every box in the **answer_boxes** list on the screen and colors them all orange.

10 **Try it out**
Save your file and run it from the command line in the Command Prompt or Terminal window. You should be able to see your GUI, ready to be filled with quiz questions. If your program fails to run successfully, go back to your code and try to catch those bugs!

I'm not sure how to run the game! Better check pages 24–25 for help.

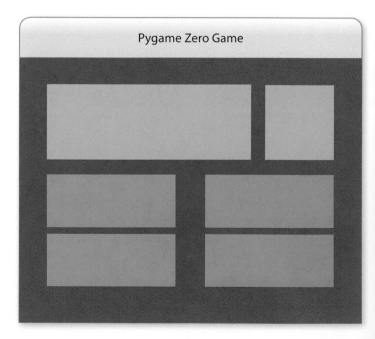

Pygame Zero Game

11 Set the score

Now that the interface is ready, you need to start thinking about how the game will work. Create a variable to hold the score and set it to zero. Type this after the code you wrote in Step 8.

```
answer_boxes = [answer_box1, answer_box2, answer_box3, answer_box4]

score = 0
```

Don't forget to save your work.

12 Set the timer

You also need to create a timer that will hold the number of seconds the player has left to answer each question. You can give them ten seconds to answer by setting the variable to **10**.

```
score = 0
time_left = 10
```

This is the number of seconds the player has to answer each question.

13 Add the first question

It's time to create the first quiz question. All the questions will be multiple choice, which means there are several possible answers, but only one of them is correct. You can use a list to store the information about each question. Type this code next.

This is the name of the list. Here it means question 1.

This question is the first item in the list.

```
time_left = 10

q1 = ["What is the capital of France?",
      "London", "Paris", "Berlin", "Tokyo", 2]
```

These are all the possible answers to the question.

This number indicates the position of the correct answer. Here it's **2**, which means **Paris** is the correct answer.

14 More questions

Let's add some more questions by typing the code shown in black below the lines from Step 13. Remember, you can create your own sets of questions if you like. You could base them on your favorite sports team, or show off what you know about your favorite series of books.

Any questions?

```
q1 = ["What is the capital of France?",
      "London", "Paris", "Berlin", "Tokyo", 2]

q2 = ["What is 5+7?",
      "12", "10", "14", "8", 1]

q3 = ["What is the seventh month of the year?",
      "April", "May", "June", "July", 4]

q4 = ["Which planet is closest to the Sun?",
      "Saturn", "Neptune", "Mercury", "Venus", 3]

q5 = ["Where are the pyramids?",
      "India", "Egypt", "Morocco", "Canada", 2]
```

15 Create a list for the questions

Next you need to add some code to keep the questions in order. You can do this using a list, just like you did for the answer boxes in Step 8. Add this line under the code from Step 14.

```
q5 = ["Where are the pyramids?",
      "India", "Egypt", "Morocco", "Canada", 2]

questions = [q1, q2, q3, q4, q5]
```

This list holds all the questions.

16 Add a function

In a real-life quiz, the quizmaster begins by picking up the first question from the top of a list. In Python, you can do the same thing by using the **pop()** function. This function removes the first item from the list, which makes the second item move to the top of the list. So in your code, **pop()** will remove **q1**, and **q2** will take its place. Type this code next.

```
questions = [q1, q2, q3, q4, q5]
question = questions.pop(0)
```

This gets the first question from the **questions** list and stores it in a variable called **question**.

EXPERT TIPS

Pop the stack

When you place items in a list, Python stacks them on top of each other. The first item in the list appears at the top of the stack. Using the **pop()** function removes an item from the top of the stack.

17 Display the boxes

Now you need to update the **draw()** function to display the questions and the timer on the screen. Use a **for** loop to draw the possible answers inside the answer boxes. Add this code to the **draw()** function under what you typed in Step 9.

```
screen.draw.filled_rect(main_box, "sky blue")
screen.draw.filled_rect(timer_box, "sky blue")

for box in answer_boxes:
    screen.draw.filled_rect(box, "orange")

screen.draw.textbox(str(time_left), timer_box, color=("black"))
screen.draw.textbox(question[0], main_box, color=("black"))

index = 1
for box in answer_boxes:
    screen.draw.textbox(question[index], box, color=("black"))
    index = index + 1
```

This line displays the number of seconds remaining in the timer box.

This displays the question in the main box.

These lines draw each possible answer in an answer box.

18 Run the code again

Save your code and run it from the command line again. You should see the first question and its four possible answers. At the moment, you can't click on any of the options, and the timer is also fixed at ten. You'll add the code to do these things soon.

The first question is displayed on screen.

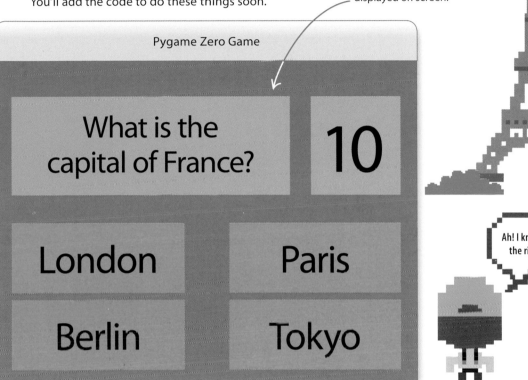

Pygame Zero Game

What is the capital of France?

10

London

Paris

Berlin

Tokyo

Ah! I knew this was the right place!

19 Set up the final screen

It's time to think about how the game should end. Write some code that displays the final score when the game ends. Replace **pass** under **def game_over()** from Step 3 with this code.

This creates a message that will show the player's final score.

```
def game_over():
    global question, time_left
    message = "Game over. You got %s questions correct" % str(score)
    question = [message, "-", "-", "-", "-", 5]
    time_left = 0
```

Since there's no correct answer here, it's set to **5**, which isn't on the list.

This sets the time to zero when the game ends.

The final message is displayed instead of another question. This will set all possible answers to a dash because you don't want the player to be able to answer.

20 Correct answers

Now you need to tell Python what you want the program to do if the player gets an answer correct. You need to increase the current score, and then get the next question. If there aren't any questions left, the game should end. Replace **pass** under **def correct_answer()** from Step 3 with this code.

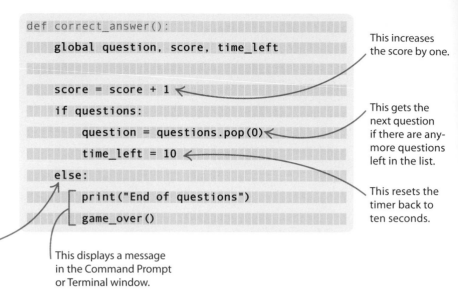

```python
def correct_answer():
    global question, score, time_left


    score = score + 1
    if questions:
        question = questions.pop(0)
        time_left = 10
    else:
        print("End of questions")
        game_over()
```

This increases the score by one.

This gets the next question if there are any-more questions left in the list.

This resets the timer back to ten seconds.

This block runs if there are no more questions in the list.

This displays a message in the Command Prompt or Terminal window.

21 Answering questions

Next add some code that will run when the player clicks on an answer box. This code will check to see which box has been clicked on, and then print the result in the Command Prompt or Terminal window. Replace **pass** under the **on_mouse_down(pos)** function from Step 3 with this code.

This line checks which box has been clicked on.

The variable **index** holds a number that represents the position of the answer box in the list.

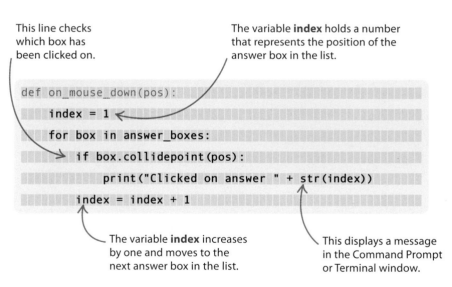

```python
def on_mouse_down(pos):
    index = 1
    for box in answer_boxes:
        if box.collidepoint(pos):
            print("Clicked on answer " + str(index))
        index = index + 1
```

The variable **index** increases by one and moves to the next answer box in the list.

This displays a message in the Command Prompt or Terminal window.

22 Click the boxes

Run your code again and click on each answer box that appears on the screen. You should see messages in the Command Prompt or Terminal window telling you which box you clicked on.

```
🏠 Rabiahma – bash – 80x24

Clicked on answer 1
Clicked on answer 2
Clicked on answer 3
Clicked on answer 4
```

23 Check the answer

Now you need to update the body of the **on_mouse_down(pos)** function from Step 21. Add the following code that will run if the player clicks on a box with the correct answer.

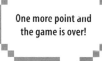

Wow! Tina has gotten all the answers correct!

```
def on_mouse_down(pos):
    index = 1
    for box in answer_boxes:
        if box.collidepoint(pos):
            print("Clicked on answer " + str(index))
            if index == question[5]:
                print("You got it correct!")
                correct_answer()
        index = index + 1
```

This checks if the player has clicked on the correct answer box.

The Item at position five in each question list is the number that corresponds to the correct answer.

24 End the game

If the player clicks on a wrong answer, the game should end. Update the code under **def on_mouse_down(pos)** one last time and use an **else** statement to run the **game_over()** function if the player selects a wrong answer. Add the code shown in black below.

One more point and the game is over!

```
def on_mouse_down(pos):
    index = 1
    for box in answer_boxes:
        if box.collidepoint(pos):
            print("Clicked on answer " + str(index))
            if index == question[5]:
                print("You got it correct!")
                correct_answer()
            else:
                game_over()
        index = index + 1
```

This block runs if the box clicked on doesn't hold the correct answer.

25 Update the timer
Now you need to update the code under **def update_time_left()** from Step 3. This will decrease the number of seconds by one every time the function is run. Type the following code.

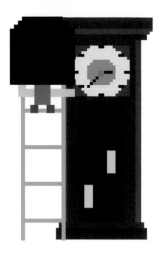

If there's still time left on the timer, this decreases it by one.

This ends the game when the time runs out.

```
def update_time_left():
    global time_left

    if time_left:
        time_left = time_left - 1
    else:
        game_over()
```

26 Schedule the timer
Finally, you need to update the **update_time_left()** function so that it runs automatically once every second. You can use Pygame Zero's clock tool to do this. Add this line of code to the very bottom of your program.

This calls the **update_time_left()** function once every second.

```
    global time_left

    if time_left:
        time_left = time_left - 1
    else:
        game_over()

clock.schedule_interval(update_time_left, 1.0)
```

27 Get quizzing!
That's it! Run your game and try it out. Hopefully, you'll be able to answer all the questions correctly. Remember, if your screen doesn't look right, you'll have to go back to your code and debug it. Read every line carefully and make sure your code matches the steps exactly. Have fun quizzing your friends!

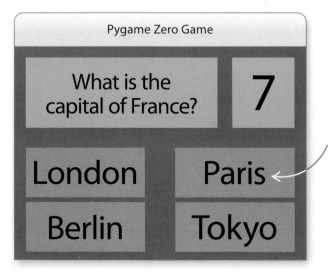

Pygame Zero Game

What is the capital of France?

7

London   Paris

Berlin   Tokyo

The player needs to click on the correct answer before the time runs out.

Hacks and tweaks

You've built a great game, but don't limit yourself to just five questions. Take Big Quiz to the next level by tweaking some of its rules. Here are some suggestions to get you started.

Got it!

▷ **Take the hint**
You can give the player a hint by displaying the correct answer box in the Command Prompt or Terminal window if they press the **H** key. Here is some code you could use to do this.

```
def on_key_up(key):
    if key == keys.H:
        print("The correct answer is box number %s " % question[5])
```

```
def on_key_up(key):
    global score
    if key == keys.H:
        print("The correct answer is box number %s " % question[5])
    if key == keys.SPACE:
        score = score - 1
        correct_answer()
```

This block first decreases the player's score by one and then runs the **correct_answer()** function, which increases it by one, keeping the score the same.

◁ **Skip a question**
You could add some more code to the **on_key_up(key)** function that allows the player to skip a question by pressing the **Space bar**. Skipping a question means they move on to the next question, but without scoring a point. Here's one way of doing it.

▷ **More questions**
You can play this game over and over again, but to keep it interesting, you can change the questions or even add some more. Here are a few examples of questions that you might want to use. You can always add some of your own! If you add extra questions, what else in the code will you need to update?

```
q6 = ["What is a quarter of 200?",
      "50", "100", "25", "150", 1]


q7 = ["Which is the largest state in the USA?",
      "Wyoming", "Alaska", "Florida", "Texas", 2]


q8 = ["How many wives did Henry VIII have?",
      "Eight", "Four", "Six", "One", 3]
```

▷ **Dash of color**

You can make your interface more attractive by changing the color of the background, the boxes, or the text that appears on screen. Here are some colors along with their RGB values that you can play with. Take a look at page 75 to find out how RGB values work.

papaya whip
(R 255, G 239, B 213)

plum
(R 221, G 160, B 221)

slate blue
(R 106, G 90, B 205)

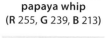
moccasin
(R 255, G 228, B 181)

orchid
(R 218, G 112, B 214)

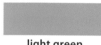
dark slate blue
(R 72, G 61, B 139)

light salmon
(R 255, G 160, B 122)

hot pink
(R 255, G 105, B 180)

peach puff
(R 255, G 218, B 185)

fuchsia
(R 255, G 0, B 255)

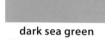
pale green
(R 152, G 251, B 152)

salmon
(R 250, G 128, B 114)

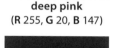
deep pink
(R 255, G 20, B 147)

pale goldenrod
(R 238, G 232, B 170)

medium orchid
(R 186, G 85, B 211)

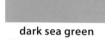
light green
(R 144, G 238, B 144)

light coral
(R 240, G 128, B 128)

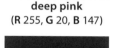
medium violet red
(R 199, G 21, B 133)

yellow
(R 255, G 255, B 0)

blue violet
(R 138, G 43, B 226)

dark sea green
(R 143, G 188, B 143)

crimson
(R 220, G 20, B 60)

coral
(R 255, G 127, B 80)

gold
(R 255, G 215, B 0)

dark violet
(R 148, G 0, B 211)

green yellow
(R 173, G 255, B 47)

red
(R 255, G 0, B 0)

tomato
(R 255, G 99, B 71)

khaki
(R 240, G 230, B 140)

dark orchid
(R 153, G 50, B 204)

chartreuse
(R 127, G 255, B 0)

fire brick
(R 178, G 34, B 34)

orange red
(R 255, G 69, B 0)

dark khaki
(R 189, G 183, B 107)

dark magenta
(R 139, G 0, B 139)

lawn green
(R 124, G 252, B 0)

dark red
(R 139, G 0, B 0)

dark orange
(R 255, G 140, B 0)

lavender
(R 230, G 230, B 250)

purple
(R 128, G 0, B 128)

lime
(R 0, G 255, B 0)

pale violet red
(R 219, G 112, B 147)

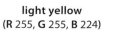
orange
(R 255, G 165, B 0)

thistle
(R 216, G 191, B 216)

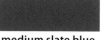
indigo
(R 75, G 0, B 130)

lime green
(R 50, G 205, B 50)

pink
(R 255, G 192, B 203)

light yellow
(R 255, G 255, B 224)

violet
(R 238, G 130, B 238)

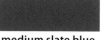
medium slate blue
(R 123, G 104, B 238)

sea green
(R 46, G 139, B 87)

green
(R 0, G 128, B 0)

pale turquoise
(R 175, G 238, B 238)

royal blue
(R 65, G 105, B 225)

rosy brown
(R 188, G 143, B 143)

maroon
(R 128, G 0, B 0)

dark green
(R 0, G 100, B 0)

sky blue
(R 135, G 206, B 235)

medium blue
(R 0, G 0, B 205)

burly wood
(R 222, G 184, B 135)

azure
(R 240, G 255, B 255)

olive drab
(R 107, G 142, B 35)

light sky blue
(R 135, G 206, B 250)

dark blue
(R 0, G 0, B 139)

tan
(R 210, G 180, B 140)

gainsboro
(R 220, G 220, B 220)

olive
(R 128, G 128, B 0)

cyan
(R 0, G 255, B 255)

navy
(R 0, G 0, B 128)

sandy brown
(R 244, G 164, B 96)

light gray
(R 211, G 211, B 211)

dark olive green
(R 85, G 107, B 47)

medium turquoise
(R 72, G 209, B 204)

midnight blue
(R 25, G 25, B 112)

goldenrod
(R 218, G 165, B 32)

silver
(R 192, G 192, B 192)

spring green
(R 0, G 255, B 127)

turquoise
(R 64, G 224, B 208)

corn silk
(R 255, G 248, B 220)

peru
(R 205, G 133, B 63)

dark gray
(R 169, G 169, B 169)

dark cyan
(R 0, G 139, B 139)

cadet blue
(R 95, G 158, B 160)

beige
(R 245, G 245, B 220)

dark goldenrod
(R 184, G 134, B 11)

gray
(R 128, G 128, B 128)

teal
(R 0, G 128, B 128)

deep sky blue
(R 0, G 191, B 255)

linen
(R 250, G 240, B 230)

chocolate
(R 210, G 105, B 30)

dim gray
(R 105, G 105, B 105)

medium aquamarine
(R 102, G 205, B 170)

dodger blue
(R 30, G 144, B 255)

antique white
(R 250, G 235, B 215)

saddle brown
(R 139, G 69, B 19)

slate gray
(R 112, G 128, B 144)

light sea green
(R 32, G 178, B 170)

steel blue
(R 70, G 130, B 180)

wheat
(R 245, G 222, B 179)

sienna
(R 160, G 82, B 45)

light slate gray
(R 119, G 136, B 153)

light cyan
(R 224, G 255, B 255)

medium slate blue
(R 123, G 104, B 238)

misty rose
(R 255, G 228, B 225)

brown
(R 165, G 42, B 42)

black
(R 0, G 0, B 0)

Balloon Flight

How to build Balloon Flight

Take control of your own hot-air balloon and try to avoid the obstacles that come your way as you fly.

What happens

When the game starts, a hot-air balloon appears in the middle of the screen. You need to use the mouse button to make the balloon rise or fall. The challenge is to keep the balloon in the air without hitting any birds, houses, or trees. For every obstacle you avoid, you'll score one point. But as soon as you hit one, the game is over.

◁ **Balloon**
The balloon begins to drop as soon as the game starts. You can make it rise again by clicking the mouse.

◁ **Obstacles**
The obstacles keep appearing at random positions. The player needs to avoid all the obstacles to stay in the game.

A cloudy backdrop sets the scene.

Pygame Zero Game

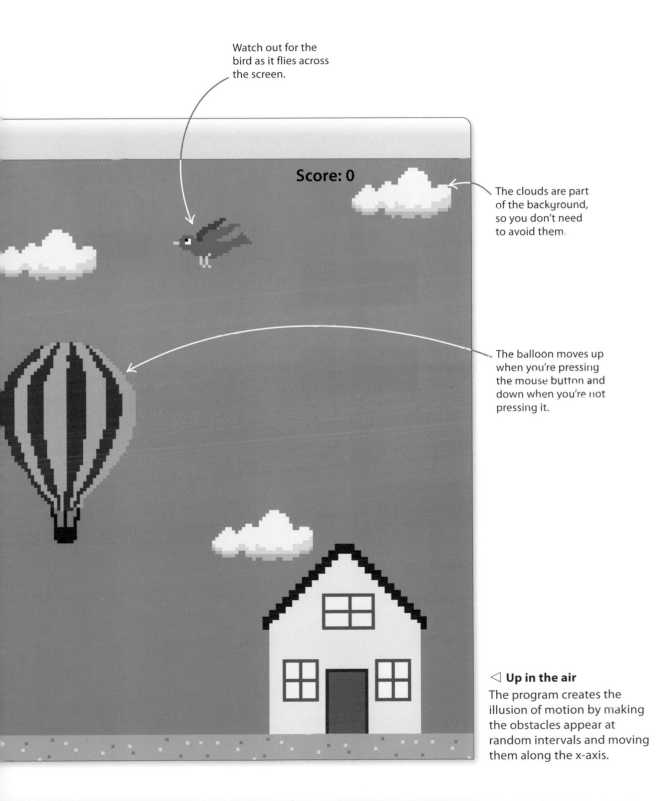

Watch out for the bird as it flies across the screen.

Score: 0

The clouds are part of the background, so you don't need to avoid them.

The balloon moves up when you're pressing the mouse button and down when you're not pressing it.

◁ **Up in the air**
The program creates the illusion of motion by making the obstacles appear at random intervals and moving them along the x-axis.

How it works

First you'll add the balloon and all the obstacles to the code. The program will check if the player has pressed the mouse button to move the balloon up, or hasn't to let it fall. Once an obstacle has disappeared off the left edge of the screen, the program will place a new one up to 800 pixels off the right edge of the screen at a random position to make the obstacles appear at random intervals. If the balloon hits any of the obstacles, the game will end and the top scores will be displayed.

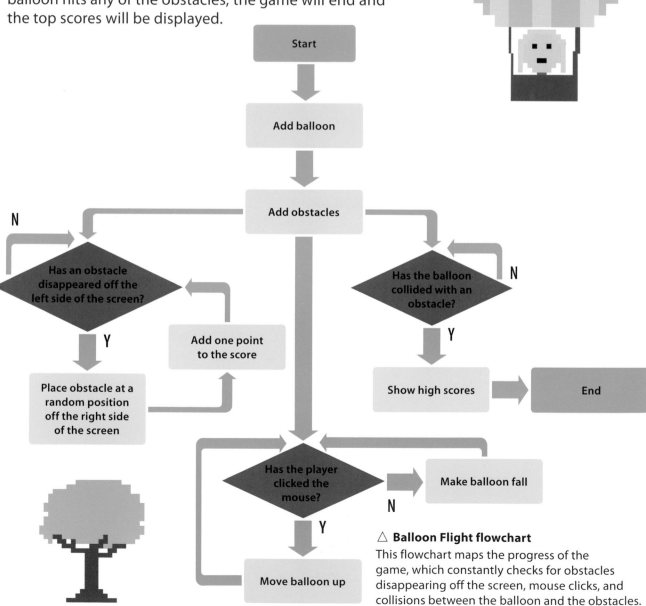

Start

Add balloon

Add obstacles

N

Has an obstacle disappeared off the left side of the screen?

Y

Place obstacle at a random position off the right side of the screen

Add one point to the score

Has the balloon collided with an obstacle?

N

Y

Show high scores

End

Has the player clicked the mouse?

N

Make balloon fall

Y

Move balloon up

△ **Balloon Flight flowchart**
This flowchart maps the progress of the game, which constantly checks for obstacles disappearing off the screen, mouse clicks, and collisions between the balloon and the obstacles.

Up, up, and away!

Before you take to the skies, it's important to understand the key elements used to build this game. The code is a bit long and tricky, so be extra careful when you're typing it out.

1 First steps

Go to the python-games folder you made earlier and create a folder called *balloon-flight* inside it. Now open IDLE and create an empty file by going to the **File** menu and choosing **New File**. Save this file as *balloon.py* in the balloon-flight folder.

Save As:	balloon.py
Tags:	
Where:	📁 balloon-flight

Cancel   Save

2 Set up an images folder

This game uses six images. Create a new folder called *images* within your balloon-flight folder. Find the Balloon Flight images in the Python Games Resource Pack (**dk.com/computercoding**) and copy them into the images folder as shown here.

balloon-flight
- balloon.py
- images
  - background.png
  - balloon.png
  - bird-down.png
  - bird-up.png
  - house.png
  - tree.png

3 Create a file to store the high scores

Next open a new file in IDLE and type the following code in it. From the **File** menu, select **Save As...** and save the file as *high-scores.txt* in the balloon-flight folder. Make sure you delete the .py extension.

```
0 0 0
```
Make sure you put a space between each **0**.

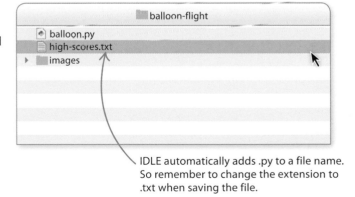

balloon-flight
- balloon.py
- high-scores.txt
- images

IDLE automatically adds .py to a file name. So remember to change the extension to .txt when saving the file.

4 Import a module

Now that your folders are ready, it's time to start writing the code. First you need to import a module that's used in the program. Type this line at the top of your balloon.py IDLE file.

```
from random import randint
```

This function will be used to generate random positions for the obstacles on the screen.

5 Set the screen size

Next you need to set the size of the screen for your game. Type this code under the line from Step 4.

```
WIDTH = 800
HEIGHT = 600
```

This sets the screen size in pixels.

6 Get the balloon ready

Now you need to set up the Actors. First add the hot-air balloon, which the player controls to play the game.

```
balloon = Actor("balloon")
balloon.pos = 400, 300
```

This line creates a new Actor using the balloon image.

This line places the balloon in the center of the screen.

7 Prepare the obstacles

Next you need to set up the Actors for all the obstacles in the game. Create one for the bird, one for the house, and one for the tree.

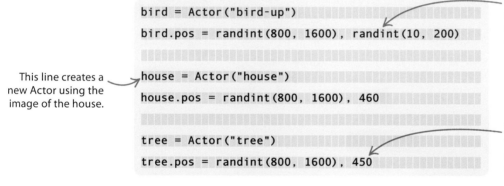

```
bird = Actor("bird-up")
bird.pos = randint(800, 1600), randint(10, 200)

house = Actor("house")
house.pos = randint(800, 1600), 460

tree = Actor("tree")
tree.pos = randint(800, 1600), 450
```

This line makes the bird appear at a random position on the x-axis between 800 and 1600 pixels, and at a random position on the y-axis between 10 and 200 pixels.

This line creates a new Actor using the image of the house.

This value makes the tree appear on the grass at the bottom of the screen.

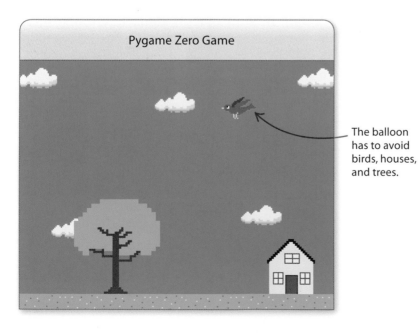

Pygame Zero Game

The balloon has to avoid birds, houses, and trees.

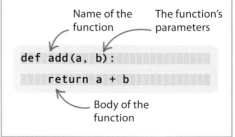

EXPERT TIPS

Functions

A function is made up of two parts—a header and a body. The header is the first line of the function that includes the name and any parameters it has. The body is the code that the function runs when it's called.

Name of the function

The function's parameters

```
def add(a, b):
    return a + b
```

Body of the function

8 Create global variables

You can now set up the global variables. Add these lines after the code from Step 7.

This keeps track of the image used for the bird Actor. The image will be changed later in the game to make the bird look like it's flapping its wings.

```
tree.pos = randint(800, 1600), 450

bird_up = True
up = False
game_over = False
score = 0
number_of_updates = 0

scores = []
```

This line keeps track of the player's score.

This list stores the top three high scores for the game.

This variable keeps track of how many times the game has been updated to change the image of the bird.

9 Manage the high scores

Next add placeholders for the functions that will manage the high scores. You will need a function to update the scores and another to display them. The bodies of these functions will be added later on.

```
scores = []

def update_high_scores():
    pass

def display_high_scores():
    pass
```

Use **pass** to create a function placeholder. You can define it later.

. . ▪ EXPERT TIPS

Obstacles on screen

In Balloon Flight, the balloon stays in the middle of the screen and the obstacles move past it. This makes it look like it's the balloon that's moving. To make the obstacles appear at random intervals, the game chooses a random position for each one to appear between 800 and 1600 pixels. Because the width of the screen is 800 pixels, the obstacles will first "appear" off screen, so you won't see them right away. Later on, you'll add code to make these obstacles move from right to left, so the farther off screen an obstacle is placed, the longer it will take to appear on screen. The upper limit is set to 1600 because otherwise the obstacles would take too long to appear.

The position of the house on the y-axis is fixed at 460.

```
house.pos = randint(800, 1600), 460
```

The house can appear anywhere along the x-axis between 800 and 1600 pixels.

I must steer clear of all these obstacles!

10 **Create the draw() function**
Just like in the other games you've created, you now
need to add a **draw()** function to your code. You will also
add an image for the game background instead of just a
solid color. Add these lines after the code from Step 9.

This adds a background
image of the sky, grass,
and clouds.

```
def draw():
    screen.blit("background", (0, 0))
    if not game_over:
        balloon.draw()
        bird.draw()
        house.draw()
        tree.draw()
        screen.draw.text("Score: " + str(score), (700, 5), color="black")
```

This line displays
the score on screen.

If the game isn't over, this code
will draw the Actors on screen.

11 **Show high scores**
In the **draw()** function, you need to add
a call to **display_high_scores()** when the
game is over. Type this immediately after
the last line of code from Step 10.

```
    else:
        display_high_scores()
```

Remember to add four
spaces before **else**.

This won't do anything yet
because you haven't written
the body of this function.

12 **Test your code**
Now try running your code. You should see the
balloon in the middle of the screen and a current
score of zero. There won't be any obstacles on
the screen yet—these will only appear once
you've added some code to make them move
onto the screen.

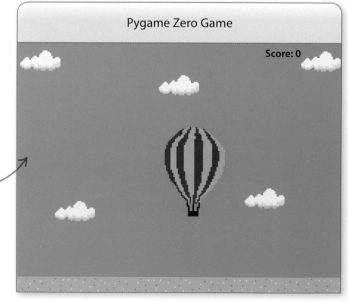

You can see the
background used
in the game.

Coordinates

In most programming languages, the coordinates (0, 0) refer to the top-left corner of the screen. Subtracting 50 pixels from the y-coordinate in **on_mouse_down()** makes the balloon go 50 pixels closer to 0 on the y-axis, which is the top of the screen. Therefore, the balloon goes up.

I can't believe this is actually working!

13 **Reacting to mouse clicks**
Now you need to define two event handler functions—**on_mouse_down()** to make the balloon rise if the player pushes down on the mouse button, and **on_mouse_up()** to let the balloon fall if they release the button. Add this code under what you typed in Step 11.

```
    else:
            display_high_scores()

def on_mouse_down():
    global up
    up = True
    balloon.y -= 50

def on_mouse_up():
    global up
    up = False
```

These functions handle the mouse button presses.

Shorthand calculations

With Python, you can perform a calculation using a variable and then store the result in the same variable. For example, to add 1 to a variable called **a**, you would usually write: **a = a + 1**.

A shorter way to write this calculation and still get the same result is **a += 1**. You can also do this with subtraction, multiplication, and division. For example:

a = a - 1 is the same as **a -= 1**
a = a / 1 is the same as **a /= 1**
a = a * 1 is the same as **a *= 1**

Quick! What's 4 + 4?

14 Make the bird flap
To make the bird more realistic, add a function to make it look like it's flapping its wings. You don't need to do this for the other obstacles.

```
def flap():
    global bird_up
    if bird_up:
        bird.image = "bird-down"
        bird_up = False
    else:
        bird.image = "bird-up"
        bird_up = True
```

If the bird's wings are up, this code will change its image to the one where the bird's wings are down.

EXPERT TIPS
Actor animations

You can make your Actors look like they're moving by using two or more different images of the same Actor. For example, in this game, there are two images of a bird—one with its wings up and one with its wings down. By alternating between the two images, it looks as if the bird is flapping its wings. The same function could make a person look like they're dancing, or a frog look like it's jumping!

15 Create the update() function
Now you need to create a function to update the game. Remember, **update()** is a built-in function that automatically runs 60 times a second, so you don't need to call it. Add this code right after the lines from Step 14.

```
def update():
    global game_over, score, number_of_updates
```

This line declares the variables the function must change.

16 Add in gravity
Next add some code to make the balloon move down when the player isn't pressing the mouse button. Add this code to the **update()** function from Step 15.

```
    global game_over, score, number_of_updates
    if not game_over:
        if not up:
            balloon.y += 1
```

If the mouse button is not being pressed, this moves the balloon down by one pixel.

17 Test your code
Let's run the code again. This time you'll see the same screen as in Step 12, but the balloon should react to mouse clicks.

18 Move the bird

Next you need to add some code to make it look like the bird is flying across the screen while flapping its wings. This code will move the bird to the left by four pixels to make it seem like it's flying across the screen.

If the bird is on the screen, this will move it to the left.

```
        balloon.y += 1

    if bird.x > 0:
        bird.x -= 4
        if number_of_updates == 9:
            flap()
            number_of_updates = 0
        else:
            number_of_updates += 1
```

This block of code will make the bird flap its wings every tenth time the **update()** function is called.

Get out of the way!

19 Handle the bird flying off the screen

When the bird disappears off the left edge of the screen, you need to move it back to a random position off the right side of the screen, just like you did at the beginning of the game. The height at which the bird appears also needs to be randomly chosen. Type the following code immediately after the last line of code in Step 18.

Remember to add eight spaces before typing this line.

This code places the bird at a random position off the right side of the screen.

```
        else:
            number_of_updates += 1
    else:
        bird.x = randint(800, 1600)
        bird.y = randint(10, 200)
        score += 1
        number_of_updates = 0
```

This adds one to the player's score for every obstacle that disappears off the screen.

EXPERT TIPS

Smooth animations

In Python, the **update()** function is automatically called 60 times every second. If you change the image of the bird each time this function is called, it would just be a blur on the screen. To make the animation smoother, add a block of code that will change the image every tenth time the function is called. You can change this interval if you want. But if the gap between the updates is too big, the bird will appear to move very slowly.

Dude, you're so wrong! The actors aren't blurry at all!

20 **Move the house**

Just like you made the bird move across the screen, you now need to make the house move, too. Add this code under the lines from Step 19.

```
        else:
            bird.x = randint(800, 1600)
            bird.y = randint(10, 200)
            score += 1
            number_of_updates = 0

    if house.right > 0:
        house.x -= 2
    else:
        house.x = randint(800, 1600)
        score += 1
```

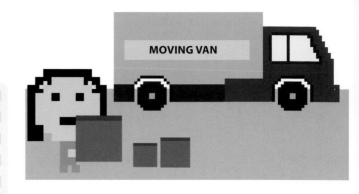

MOVING VAN

If the house disappears off the left edge of the screen, this line places it at a random position off the right edge.

This line will update the score by one if the house moves off the screen.

21 **Move the tree**

Using the same logic as before, add these lines under the code from Step 20 to make the tree move across the screen.

Don't forget to count the number of spaces before each line of code.

```
        else:
            house.x = randint(400, 800)
            score += 1

    if tree.right > 0:
        tree.x -= 2
    else:
        tree.x = randint(800, 1600)
        score += 1
```

EXPERT TIPS

Scrolling across the screen

Once the obstacles disappear off the screen, you need to move them back to the right-hand side of the screen. This is to create the illusion of motion and make it look like lots of obstacles are appearing on the screen when, in reality, you only use one Actor for each type of obstacle in your code. Scrolling the same Actor across the screen means you don't have to create new Actors every time one disappears off the screen.

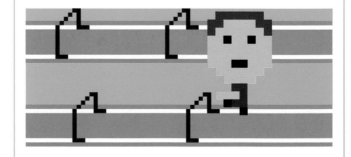

22 Keep it steady

Your game needs to end if the balloon hits the top or the bottom of the screen. Type this code under the lines from Step 21.

```
score += 1


        if balloon.top < 0 or balloon.bottom > 560:
            game_over = True
            update_high_scores()
```

This line checks if the balloon has touched the top or bottom of the screen.

23 Handle collisions with obstacles

Finally, you need to add some code to end the game if the balloon hits any of the three obstacles. Add the code below.

This checks if the balloon has hit any of the three obstacles.

```
        update_high_scores()


        if balloon.collidepoint(bird.x, bird.y) or \
        balloon.collidepoint(house.x, house.y) or \
        balloon.collidepoint(tree.x, tree.y):
            game_over = True
            update_high_scores()
```

This sets **game_over** to True, which tells the program that the game is over.

This updates the high scores, if necessary.

Use a backslash character if you need to split a long line of code over more than one line.

24 Test your code

Save your program and run it from the command line. You should now be able to play the game, but it's not quite finished yet! Next you'll find out how to add high scores to your game.

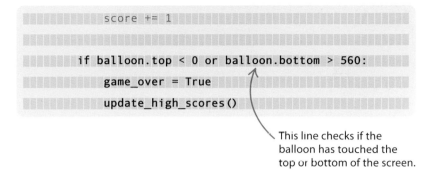

Pygame Zero Game

Score: 0

All the obstacles will now seem to move across the screen.

25 **Update the high scores**
Now go back to the **update_high_scores()** function from Step 9 and write the body. This function gets the top three high scores and updates them if the player's current score has beaten one of them. Replace **pass** with the code in black below, then carefully follow the extra instructions to get the path for your high-score.txt file.

```
def update_high_scores():
    global score, scores
    filename = r"/Users/bharti/Desktop/python-games/balloon-flight/high-scores.txt"
    scores = []
```

This resets the list of high scores.

You will need to change this gray bit of code to the high-scores.txt file's location on your own computer. Drag the high-scores.txt file into the Command Prompt or Terminal window, then copy and paste the path here and put quotation marks around it. Replace any backslashes \ that look out of place with a space.

26 **Get the current high scores**
To know if the player's score has beaten any of the previous scores, you'll need to read the scores saved in the high-scores.txt file you created in Step 3. Add this code under the lines from Step 25.

This opens the high-scores.txt file for reading.

```
    scores = []
    with open(filename, "r") as file:
        line = file.readline()
        high_scores = line.split()
```

Remember, the high scores file only has one line. This reads the single line stored in the file.

This function splits the high scores stored in one line into three different strings.

Splitting strings

In this game, all the high scores are saved in a text file on a single line as a string. To check if the player has beaten any of these high scores, you need to split this string into three separate parts. Python's **split()** function can be used to split a string at a character and then store the separate strings in a list. You can pass a parameter to the **split()** function telling it which character you want to split the string by.

```
name = "Martin,Craig,Daniel,Claire"
name.split(",")
```

This parameter splits the string at each comma. If you don't provide a parameter, the function will split the string at the space character, like in Step 26 of your program.

The list is returned with four separate strings.

```
["Martin", "Craig", "Daniel", "Claire"]
```

EXPERT TIPS

Keeping score

Imagine the current high scores are 12, 10, 8, and a player scores 11. If your code just replaced each score you've beaten with the new score, you'd end up with 12, 11, 11, which wouldn't be right. To avoid this, your code needs to compare the player's score with the top score first. 11 is less than 12, so it doesn't replace it. It then needs to move on to the second-highest score. The next one, 11 is greater than 10, so it replaces it. Now that 11 is on the scoreboard, the code needs to check if 10, the score that was just replaced, is greater than the score currently in third place. Because 10 is greater than 8, it replaces it, and 8 is removed altogether.

12 10 8 ← This is an example of an existing list of scores.

12 11 8 ← Once 11 has replaced 10, you need to check 10, rather than 11, against 8.

12 11 10 ← These are the new three high scores.

27 **Find the highest scores**
Now write some code that will check if the current score has beaten any of the three high scores. Add this code under the lines from Step 26.

This loops through the list of high scores.

```
            high_scores = line.split()
            for high_score in high_scores:
                if(score > int(high_score)):
                    scores.append(str(score) + " ")
                    score = int(high_score)
                else:
                    scores.append(str(high_score) + " ")
```

This checks if the player's score is higher than the existing high scores.

This sets **score** to the high score that was just beaten.

If the player hasn't beaten the high score in question, that current high score is added to the list.

If the player's score is higher than an existing high score, this adds it to the list.

28 **Write the high scores in the file**
Use **write()** to write the new high score to the high-scores.txt file. Add this code under the code from Step 27.

```
                    scores.append(str(high_score) + " ")
            with open(filename, "w") as file:
                for high_score in scores:
                    file.write(high_score)
```

This block writes the new high scores to the .txt file.

This opens the high-scores.txt file to be written to.

File handling

In Balloon Flight, you've used a .txt file to store the high scores. A file like this can be opened and assigned to a variable. The main functions that you need to handle the file are **open()**, **read()**, and **write()**.

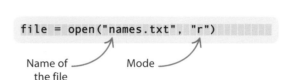

▷ **open()** takes two parameters, the file name and the "mode", which tells Python what you want to do with the file. There are four modes in Python: **r** for reading, **w** for writing, **a** for adding to the end of a file, and **r+** for reading and writing.

```
file = open("names.txt", "r")
```

Name of ⸜ the file   Mode ⸍

▽ Use the **read()** function to read an entire file.

```
names = file.read()
```

▽ You can even add all the lines to a list.

```
lines = []
for line in file:
        lines.append(line)
```

▽ You can also just read a single line, rather than the whole file.

```
name = file.readline()
```

▽ Now use the **write()** function to write to a file.

```
file = open("names.txt", "w")
file.write("Martin")
```

▽ When you're finished with a file, you should close it to tell the program you are done with it.

```
file.close()
```

It's time to close. Are you sure you're done?

▽ If you forget to close a file after using it, some of the data may not get written to it. Use the **with** statement to stop this from happening. This statement opens the file and automatically closes it when it has finished running the body of the **with** statement.

```
with open("names.txt", "r") as file:
        name = file.readline()
```

Body of the function.

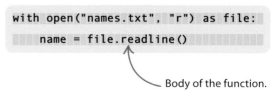

29 **Display high scores**

Now that you've written a function to collect the high scores, you need to write one to display them on the screen. Replace the word **pass** under **def display_high_scores()** from Step 9 with this code.

```
def display_high_scores():
    screen.draw.text("HIGH SCORES", (350, 150), color="black")
    y = 175
    position = 1
    for high_score in scores:
        screen.draw.text(str(position) + ". " + high_score, (350, y), color="black")
        y += 25
        position += 1
```

This sets the first high score's position on the y-axis.

This line writes HIGH SCORES on the screen.

This adds to the y position, so that each high score is displayed 25 pixels below the previous one.

This line displays the high scores on the screen.

Hacks and tweaks

There are lots of ways you can adapt this game to make it more complex. Here are some ideas you can try out.

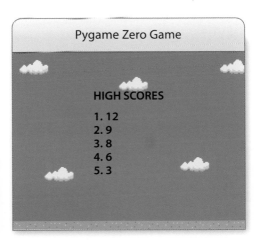

△ **More high scores**

Right now the game only stores the top three high scores. Can you change it to store the top five or ten? Remember the text file you created in Step 3 with three zeroes? How can you edit this file to store more high scores?

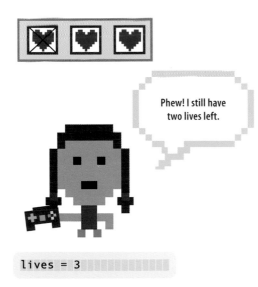

Phew! I still have two lives left.

```
lives = 3
```

△ **Lives**

Why don't you give the player some more chances to complete the game? Introduce a new variable to keep track of a player's lives. Reduce the number by one every time the player hits an obstacle. When there are no more lives left, the game ends.

```
bird.x -= 4
```

Make this number higher to increase the speed.

△ Speed it up

Do you want to make the game more challenging? Why don't you make the obstacles go faster? You can do this by changing the number of pixels the obstacles move by. If you make the bird faster, remember to also update the **flap()** function to match the new speed.

I think I read about file handling on page 132 as well.

```
new_high_score = False
```

△ File handling

In the game, you write to the high-scores.txt file every time the program exits. It would be more efficient to write to the file only if the high scores have changed. To code this, you can use a Boolean variable to track whether the high scores have changed. In programming, this is sometimes referred to as a "flag." In the game, if the flag is set to True, then the high scores have changed and you have to write them back to the file. But if there is no change, there is no need to write anything to the file.

I didn't know I could score points like this!

△ Different way to score

In the current game, the player scores a point every time an obstacle disappears off the left edge of the screen. You can change the code so that the player scores every time they pass an obstacle on the screen. Can you figure out how to do this? Remember the position of the balloon always remains at 400 pixels along the x-axis.

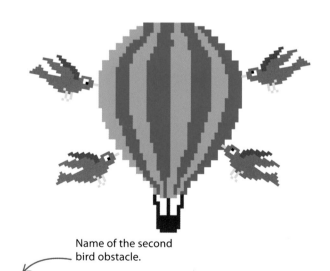

Name of the second bird obstacle.

```
bird2 = Actor("bird-up")
bird2.pos = randint(800, 1600), randint(10, 200)
```

△ Add in multiples of each obstacle

Do you find avoiding just one of each obstacle on the screen too easy? You could change the code so that more than one of each obstacle appears on the screen at the same time.

▽ **Level up**

Make the game more fun by adding levels and increasing the speed with each level. To do this, you could set the number of obstacles in each level to ten. To complete the level, the player must clear all the obstacles and score ten points. Every time the score reaches a multiple of ten, make the obstacles move faster. In the original game, the birds move by four pixels at a time, and the houses and trees move by two. If you want to increase it with every level, you need to store the speed in a variable. Just remember that the bird should always be traveling twice as fast as the trees and houses.

```
speed = 2
bird.x -= speed * 2
```

▽ **Space out the obstacles**

Sometimes all the obstacles—the tree, the house, and the bird—might appear at the same position on the x-axis. This works fine, but you may want to avoid it. Try to change the **update()** function so that the obstacles pick a new random x coordinate if there is a clash. This code will help you get started.

```
if bird.x == house.x
```

Modulo operator

When Python performs division, it ignores the remainder. But sometimes it's useful to know if there is a remainder and what it is. For example, if you want to test if the number is even, you can do so by dividing it by 2 and checking if there is a remainder. To do this, you can use the modulo operator **%**.

```
>>> print(2 % 2)
0
```

This is 0 because there is no remainder when 2 is divided by 2.

```
>>> print(3 % 2)
1
```

This is the remainder when 3 is divided by 2.

In Balloon Flight, you can use the modulo operator to know if the score is a multiple of 10, and therefore whether the player should move to the next level.

```
score % 10
```

This would return the remainder when the score is divided by 10.

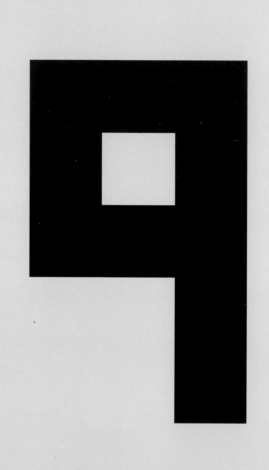

Dance Challenge

How to build Dance Challenge

Get your groove on with this fast-paced game. Watch the dancer move to the music and then put your memory skills to the test by repeating those moves. How long can you keep going without making a mistake?

What happens

In this game, the dancer performs a sequence of moves. You need to remember this sequence and make him repeat it using the four arrow keys on the keyboard.

Each correct move will earn you a point.

Pygame Zero Game

Score: 0

◁ **Dancer**
The dancer loves showing off his moves! Follow him carefully to keep on playing.

◁ **Colored squares**
One of the squares is highlighted with a yellow outline each time the dancer switches from one move to another.

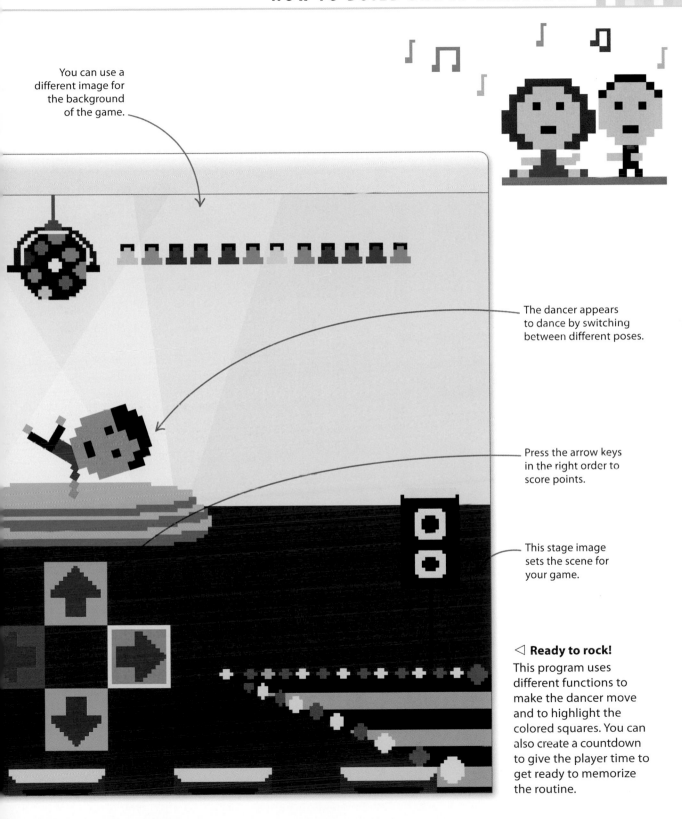

You can use a different image for the background of the game.

The dancer appears to dance by switching between different poses.

Press the arrow keys in the right order to score points.

This stage image sets the scene for your game.

◁ **Ready to rock!**
This program uses different functions to make the dancer move and to highlight the colored squares. You can also create a countdown to give the player time to get ready to memorize the routine.

How it works

You start this program by setting up functions that will generate a sequence of dance moves, create a countdown, and then display the moves on the screen. The game will keep checking if you have pressed an arrow key and if it was the correct one. If you make a mistake, the game will end.

EXPERT TIPS

Adding music

In this game, you will need to add some music for your dancer to move to. Pygame Zero has some special commands that make it quite easy to do this. Each time you add music to a game, set up a folder called *music* within your game's main folder, so that Pygame Zero knows where to find the audio files.

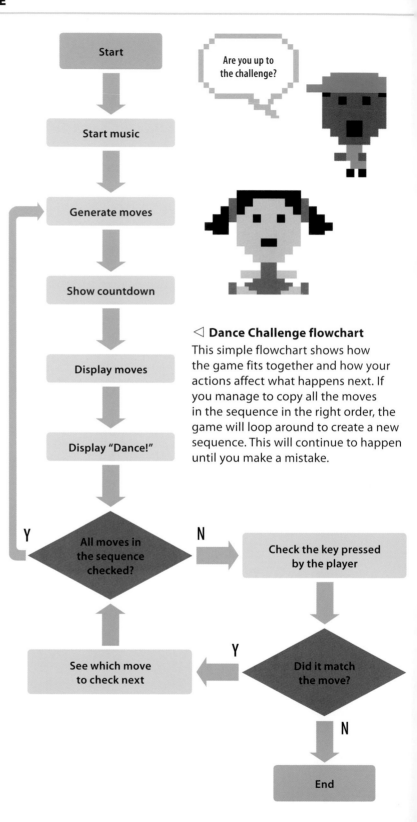

◁ **Dance Challenge flowchart**
This simple flowchart shows how the game fits together and how your actions affect what happens next. If you manage to copy all the moves in the sequence in the right order, the game will loop around to create a new sequence. This will continue to happen until you make a mistake.

Hit the dance floor

Now that you've worked out how the game will work, it's time to put your dancing shoes on and get started! Begin by setting up and saving a new file, and then import the Python modules you will need in this game. You will then use different Python functions to create the game.

 1 **Create a file in IDLE**
Open IDLE and create an empty file by going to the **File** menu and choosing **New File**.

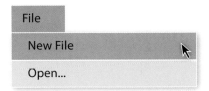

2 **Save your game**
Go to the python-games folder you made earlier. Inside this folder, create another folder called *dance-challenge* and save your IDLE file in it as *dance.py*.

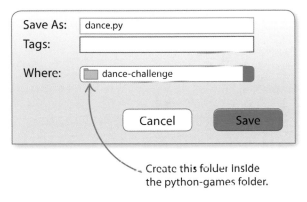

Create this folder inside the python-games folder.

 3 **Set up an image folder**
This game uses images of a dancer, a stage, and eight colored squares with an arrow inside each. You'll need to create a new folder, called *images*, inside your dance-challenge folder. This folder has to be inside the same folder as your dance.py IDLE file.

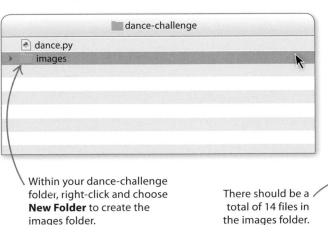

Within your dance-challenge folder, right-click and choose **New Folder** to create the images folder.

4 **Put the images into the folder**
Find the Dance Challenge files in the Python Games Resource Pack (**dk.com/computercoding**), and copy them into the images folder. Leave the .ogg audio file for the moment.

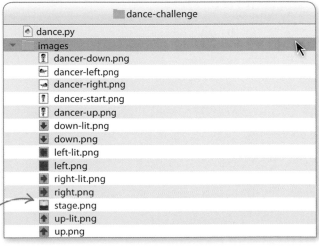

There should be a total of 14 files in the images folder.

5 Set up a music folder

This game uses an audio file so that the dancer has something to dance to. The file needs its own folder, so create a new folder called *music* inside your dance-challenge folder.

6 Put the music file into the folder

Go back to the Python Games Resource Pack, find the file called "vanishing-horizon.ogg" and copy it into the music folder. Your folders should look like this now.

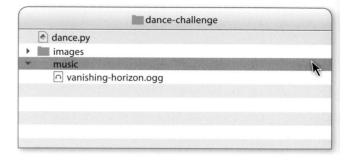

7 Import a module

Now that you're all set up, it's time to get started on the code. Open the dance.py file in IDLE and type this line of code at the top of the program. You'll use **randint()** to generate random numbers that will represent different dance moves.

```
from random import randint
```

This imports the **randint()** function from Python's Random module.

8 Set the stage

Next you need to define the global variables. These are variables that can be used in any part of the program. Add this code next.

The stage is almost set. I can't wait to get started!

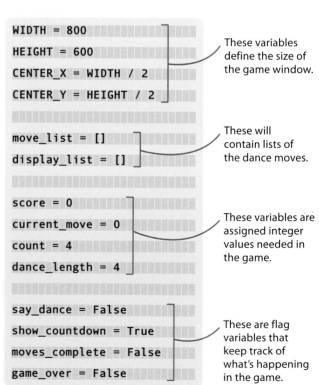

```
WIDTH = 800
HEIGHT = 600
CENTER_X = WIDTH / 2
CENTER_Y = HEIGHT / 2


move_list = []
display_list = []


score = 0
current_move = 0
count = 4
dance_length = 4


say_dance = False
show_countdown = True
moves_complete = False
game_over = False
```

These variables define the size of the game window.

These will contain lists of the dance moves.

These variables are assigned integer values needed in the game.

These are flag variables that keep track of what's happening in the game.

9 Add the Actors

Now it's time to define the Actors and set their starting positions. Add this code under what you typed in Step 8.

```
dancer = Actor("dancer-start")
dancer.pos = CENTER_X + 5, CENTER_Y - 40

up = Actor("up")
up.pos = CENTER_X, CENTER_Y + 110
right = Actor("right")
right.pos = CENTER_X + 60, CENTER_Y + 170
down = Actor("down")
down.pos = CENTER_X, CENTER_Y + 230
left = Actor("left")
left.pos = CENTER_X - 60, CENTER_Y + 170
```

When the game starts, the dancer appears in the starting position in the center of the game window.

This code will arrange the colored squares in a cross shape below the dancer.

10 Draw the Actors

It's time to see what your game is going to look like. You can display your Actors on the screen using Pygame Zero's built-in **draw()** function. Type this in next.

```
def draw():
    global game_over, score, say_dance
    global count, show_countdown
    if not game_over:
        screen.clear()
        screen.blit("stage", (0, 0))
        dancer.draw()
        up.draw()
        down.draw()
        right.draw()
        left.draw()
        screen.draw.text("Score: " +
                         str(score), color="black",
                         topleft=(10, 10))
    return
```

These lines tell Python which global variables you want to use in this function.

This command is only run if the game isn't over.

This line clears previous items drawn.

Use this function to add a background in the game window.

These lines draw all the Actors in their current positions.

This prints the score in the top-left corner of the screen.

11 Run the code

Save all the changes you've made, and then go to the command line in the Command Prompt or Terminal window. Type in **pgzrun** and drag the dance.py file into the window. Then press **Enter**.

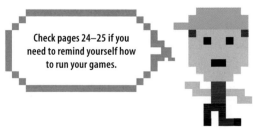

Check pages 24–25 if you need to remind yourself how to run your games.

12 First screen

If your code is working properly, your game screen should look something like this. If not, there's no need to worry. Just go back to your code and use your debugging skills to check every line for possible errors, such as spellings and number of spaces.

Take that!

13 Musical statues

You've probably spotted a problem with your dancer... he's not moving! Set up placeholders for the functions you're going to use to change that. Add this code under what you typed in Step 10.

Placeholders

Using **pass** is a good way to list all the functions you'll need so you don't forget anything.

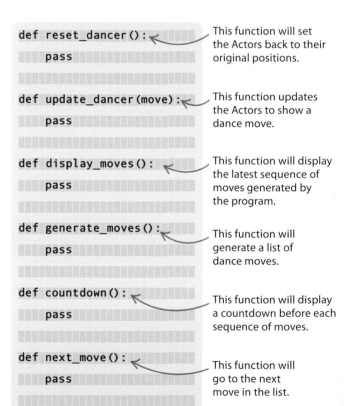

```
def reset_dancer():
    pass

def update_dancer(move):
    pass

def display_moves():
    pass

def generate_moves():
    pass

def countdown():
    pass

def next_move():
    pass

def on_key_up(key):
    pass

def update():
    pass
```

This function will set the Actors back to their original positions.

This function updates the Actors to show a dance move.

This function will display the latest sequence of moves generated by the program.

This function will generate a list of dance moves.

This function will display a countdown before each sequence of moves.

This function will go to the next move in the list.

This function will make the program react when you press a key.

This is a built-in Pygame Zero function.

14 Random numbers

Your program needs to generate dance sequences for you to memorize and repeat. The four possible moves are **Up**, **Down**, **Left**, and **Right**. You don't have a function that will generate random directions, but the **randint()** function will let you generate random numbers. If you assign each of the four moves a number, starting from 0, you will then be able to create random dance sequences. Step 15 will show you how to do this.

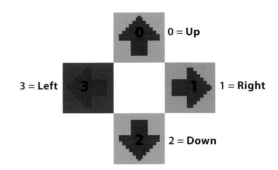

0 = Up
1 = Right
3 = Left
2 = Down

15 Let's move!

The first function you need to define properly is **update_dancer()**. This changes the image of the dancer to match the dance move he should perform. The colored square that corresponds to that dance move also changes to become outlined in yellow. Replace **pass** under the **update_dancer(move)** function from Step 13 with the code shown below. There's quite a lot to add, so be extra careful.

This function will tell the dancer which move to perform.

Don't forget to save your work.

The value in **move** tells the dancer which dance move to do. Here, it's set to **0**, which will mean **Up**.

This line tells Python which global variable to use.

This line changes the image of the dancer.

This line highlights the colored square for **Up** with a yellow outline.

The dancer will hold the move for half a second before **reset_dancer()** is called, returning him to the starting pose.

```python
def update_dancer(move):
    global game_over
    if not game_over:
        if move == 0:
            up.image = "up-lit"
            dancer.image = "dancer-up"
            clock.schedule(reset_dancer, 0.5)
        elif move == 1:
            right.image = "right-lit"
            dancer.image = "dancer-right"
            clock.schedule(reset_dancer, 0.5)
        elif move == 2:
            down.image = "down-lit"
            dancer.image = "dancer-down"
            clock.schedule(reset_dancer, 0.5)
        else:
            left.image = "left-lit"
            dancer.image = "dancer-left"
            clock.schedule(reset_dancer, 0.5)
    return
```

16 Reset the Actors

The dancer needs to return to the start position after each move. The yellow-outlined arrow square that corresponds to his dance move will also need to go back to normal. To make a function to handle this, replace the word **pass** under **def reset_dancer()** from Step 13 with this code.

```
def reset_dancer():
    global game_over
    if not game_over:
        dancer.image = "dancer-start"
        up.image = "up"
        right.image = "right"
        down.image = "down"
        left.image = "left"
    return
```

17 Make a move

Next you need to write a function that makes the dancer perform a move when you press one of the arrow keys on the keyboard. You can use Pygame Zero's built-in tool **on_key_up()** to write an event-handler function to do this. Replace **pass** under the **on_key_up(key)** function from Step 13 with this code.

```
def on_key_up(key):
    global score, game_over, move_list, current_move
    if key == keys.UP:
        update_dancer(0)
    elif key == keys.RIGHT:
        update_dancer(1)
    elif key == keys.DOWN:
        update_dancer(2)
    elif key == keys.LEFT:
        update_dancer(3)
    return
```

Each time an arrow key is pressed, the **update_dancer()** function is called with a parameter to make the dancer perform the relevant move.

18 Move those feet

It's time to see your dancer's moves! Save your file and run it from the command line. You will see the same screen as in Step 12, but this time if you hit the **Right** key, the dancer will perform the dance move assigned to that key. The square for the **Right** arrow will also get highlighted. The dancer and square will return to their starting images after half a second. Press the other arrow keys to test their moves, too.

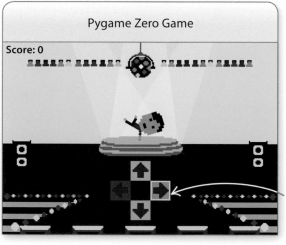

A square is highlighted to match the arrow key that you pressed.

19 Show me the steps

Now that you can make the dancer move with the arrow keys, he needs to display some computer-generated moves for the player to copy. Begin by writing the function that displays a sequence of moves to memorize. Replace **pass** under the **display_moves()** function from Step 13 with the code shown below.

Care to teach me flamenco?

```
def display_moves():
    global move_list, display_list, dance_length
    global say_dance, show_countdown, current_move
    if display_list:
        this_move = display_list[0]
        display_list = display_list[1:]
        if this_move == 0:
            update_dancer(0)
            clock.schedule(display_moves, 1)
        elif this_move == 1:
            update_dancer(1)
            clock.schedule(display_moves, 1)
        elif this_move == 2:
            update_dancer(2)
            clock.schedule(display_moves, 1)
        else:
            update_dancer(3)
            clock.schedule(display_moves, 1)
    else:
        say_dance = True
        show_countdown = False
    return
```

This line checks if the list of dance moves has something in it.

This line stores the first move in **display_list** in the variable **this_move**.

This removes the first item from **display_list** so that the second item will now be at position **0**.

If the value of **this_move** is **0**, it is passed on to this function.

This line schedules a call to the function **display_moves()** in one second.

If **display_list** is empty, this line tells the **draw()** function to display "Dance!"

This line sets the global variable **show_countdown** to False.

20 Counting down

You don't want your players to be looking away when the next set of moves to memorize is displayed. Add a function that displays *3*, *2*, and then *1* with a one-second pause between each number. You'll actually count down from *4*, but because the **countdown()** function begins by subtracting one from **count**, the number *4* doesn't appear on the screen long enough to be seen. Replace **pass** under **def countdown()** from Step 13 with this code.

```
def countdown():
    global count, game_over, show_countdown
    if count > 1:
        count = count - 1
        clock.schedule(countdown, 1)
    else:
        show_countdown = False
        display_moves()
    return
```

This updates the value in **count** by subtracting one.

This line schedules another call to the **countdown()** function in one second.

This removes the countdown from the screen if **count** is less than or equal to one.

21 Show the countdown

Now that you've defined a function for the countdown, you need to add some code to the **draw()** function to display it. You will also need to display "Dance!" when a new set of moves has been shown, so the player knows when to start entering the moves using the arrow keys. Add this code to the **draw()** function that you started in Step 10.

```
        screen.draw.text("Score: " +
                        str(score), color="black",
                        topleft=(10, 10))
    if say_dance:
        screen.draw.text("Dance!", color="black",
                        topleft=(CENTER_X - 65, 150), fontsize=60)
    if show_countdown:
        screen.draw.text(str(count), color="black",
                        topleft=(CENTER_X - 8, 150), fontsize=60)
    return
```

This line draws the word "Dance!" on the screen in black.

This line displays the current value of **count** on the screen in black.

EXPERT TIPS
Recursive functions

Both **display_moves()** and **countdown()** are functions that call themselves. These are known as recursive functions. Because Pygame Zero redraws the screen thousands of times every second, you need your recursive functions to schedule a call to themselves one whole second later. Otherwise, the moves and the countdown would be displayed too fast for even the most eagle-eyed player to see!

Can you call me back in a second?

Generate the moves

Next you need to write a function to generate a sequence of moves to display on the screen. You need to use a **for** loop to generate four random numbers ranging from **0** to **3**, where each number represents one of the moves you set up in Step 15. Each move generated will be added to two lists—**move_list** and **display_list**. Replace **pass** under **def generate_moves()** from Step 13 with this code.

This assigns values **0**, **1**, **2**, or **3** at random to the variable **rand_move**.

This line adds each new move to the end of the list of moves.

```
def generate_moves():
    global move_list, dance_length, count
    global show_countdown, say_dance
    count = 4
    move_list = []
    say_dance = False
    for move in range(0, dance_length):
        rand_move = randint(0, 3)
        move_list.append(rand_move)
        display_list.append(rand_move)
    show_countdown = True
    countdown()
    return
```

This line tells the function **draw()** to display the value in **count** to create the countdown.

23 Game over

If the player makes a mistake, you need a "GAME OVER!" message to pop up. You can do this by adding an **else** branch to the **if not game_over** statement. By doing this, if **game_over** becomes True, the dancer and squares will vanish and be replaced by the "GAME OVER!" message. Add this code to the **draw()** function immediately above the **return** statement.

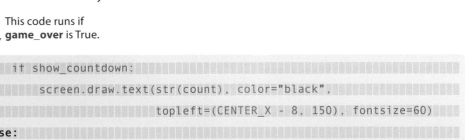

Don't forget to save your work.

This code runs if **game_over** is True.

```
    if show_countdown:
        screen.draw.text(str(count), color="black",
                         topleft=(CENTER_X - 8, 150), fontsize=60)
else:
    screen.clear()
    screen.blit("stage", (0, 0))
    screen.draw.text("Score: " +
                     str(score), color="black",
                     topleft=(10, 10))
    screen.draw.text("GAME OVER!", color="black",
                     topleft=(CENTER_X - 130, 220), fontsize=60)
    return
```

This line draws the score in the top-left corner.

This line draws "GAME OVER!" in black at the center of the screen.

24 Generation test

It's time to test your new functions and see if they are working. Add a call to **generate_moves()** just above the definition of **update()** from Step 13. Save the file and run it. You should see a countdown appear and then your dancer demonstrating a sequence of four moves. The word "Dance!" should be displayed when he's finished, but don't start dancing yet! You still need to add the code that checks if the moves entered by the player are correct.

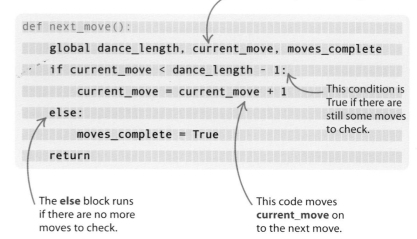

```
generate_moves()


def update():
    pass
```

The global variable **current_move** identifies which move you're dealing with.

25 Get the next move

You need a way to move along the list of moves the computer generated. This will let you compare the first move the player enters to the first move in the computer's list, and so on through the list. You also need to know when you've reached the end of the list. To do this, use the global variable **current_move** to identify which move you're dealing with. Replace **pass** under **def next_move()** from Step 13 with this code.

```
def next_move():
    global dance_length, current_move, moves_complete
    if current_move < dance_length - 1:
        current_move = current_move + 1
    else:
        moves_complete = True
    return
```

This condition is True if there are still some moves to check.

The **else** block runs if there are no more moves to check.

This code moves **current_move** on to the next move.

26 Score on each move

You now need to add some code to the **on_key_up()** function. When the player presses a key, the game needs to check whether the arrow key that's been pressed matches the move the game is currently checking. If it does, the player scores a point and **current_move** is updated to the next move on the list. If it doesn't, the game is over! Add this code to the **on_key_up(key)** function that you started in Step 17. Be careful to add it in the right place.

```
if key == keys.UP:
    update_dancer(0)
    if move_list[current_move] == 0:
        score = score + 1
        next_move()
    else:
        game_over = True
elif key == keys.RIGHT:
    update_dancer(1)
```

This block runs if the player presses the correct key.

If the player makes a mistake, **game_over** is set to True.

```
        if move_list[current_move] == 1:
            score = score + 1
            next_move()
        else:
            game_over = True
    elif key == keys.DOWN:
        update_dancer(2)
        if move_list[current_move] == 2:
            score = score + 1
            next_move()
        else:
            game_over = True
    elif key == keys.LEFT:
        update_dancer(3)
        if move_list[current_move] == 3:
            score = score + 1
            next_move()
        else:
            game_over = True
    return
```

EXPERT TIPS
Event handling

Dance Challenge uses an event handler function called **on_key_up()** to react to a player pressing an arrow key. You shouldn't put the code to deal with key presses inside the built-in **update()** function in this case because it will run too frequently. If you pressed a key down just for a second, **update()** would tell the game you had pressed it hundreds of times. This probably wouldn't match the dance sequence, so the game would finish right away.

> Don't worry!
> I'll handle it.

27 **Keep going!**
To make the game more challenging, a new set of moves needs to be displayed every time the player successfully completes a dance sequence. Replace **pass** in the **update()** function from Step 13 with the code below to do this.

> I am out of control!

```
def update():
    global game_over, current_move, moves_complete
    if not game_over:
        if moves_complete:
            generate_moves()
            moves_complete = False
            current_move = 0
```

This line runs if you complete every move in the current list.

This line generates a new series of moves and displays them.

28 Test the game

Before you add the finishing touches to your game, test it. Save your code and then run it. Try getting the first sequence of moves right to increase your score to four, then deliberately make a mistake with the second sequence. What do you see on the screen?

Pygame Zero Game

Score: 0

GAME OVER!

You passed the first test!

29 Start the music

At the moment, your dancer has nothing to dance to, which isn't much fun. Add a command in your program that will play the audio file you saved in the music folder earlier. Type this code under the command you typed in Step 24. This will tell Pygame Zero to start playing the music file until it's told to stop. If the player is still dancing at the end of the song, it will loop around and play the song again.

```
generate_moves()
music.play("vanishing-horizon")

def update():
```

30 Stop the music

You don't want the music to keep playing after the game has finished. So you need to add an **else** branch to your first **if** statement in the **update()** function to stop the music if the game is over. Add this code to what you typed in Step 27.

```
if not game_over:
    if moves_complete:
        generate_moves()
        moves_complete = False
        current_move = 0
else:
    music.stop()
```

If **game_over** is True, this line stops playing the audio file.

31 Ready to play

Your code is now complete, so get your dancing shoes on! Save the file, run it from the command line in Command Prompt or Terminal window, and see how long you can keep on dancing!

Hacks and tweaks

You can play around with the code to make the game even more interesting. But only if you've got enough energy left after all that dancing!

△ Create your own character
Make your own dancer by using the 8-bit editors available online, or use the additional images provided in the Python Games Resource Pack. You could have more than four dance moves to make more interesting and harder sequences. Just add some code under the **on_key_up()** function in Step 17 to assign keys to each of the extra moves.

△ Play against a friend!
You can play this game against a friend. Change the code so that all the odd-number sequences add to player 1's score, and the even-number ones add to player 2's score. It should show both scores at the top of the screen, and must also display a message that tells which player needs to play next, just before the countdown begins. Add some code to the **on_key_up()** function so that one player uses the keys **W**, **A**, **S**, and **D** to enter their moves, while the the other uses the **Up**, **Left**, **Down**, and **Right** keys.

```
if (rounds % 3 == 0):
    dance_length = dance_length + 1
```

△ A longer dance
You can make the game more challenging. Each time you complete three sequences, increase the **dance_length** by one. To find out how many rounds have been completed, divide the number of sequences danced by three. If the remainder is zero, then three sequences have been successfully completed since the last check, so add **1** to **dance_length**. You can use Python's modulo operator to work out the remainder. Modulo is written using the **%** symbol, so **4 % 3** will give you the remainder on dividing 4 by 3.

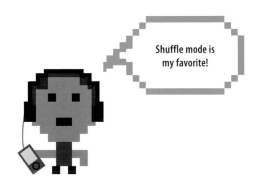

△ Change the music
You can change the game music by downloading audio files from www.creativecommons.org. Remember to look for the .ogg format. You don't have to pay for the music, but you should acknowledge the creator in your game by adding a line of code that displays the name of the track and its creators on the "GAME OVER!" screen.

Happy Garden

How to build Happy Garden

Gardening may seem like a relaxing hobby, but not in this game! Can you help a flower-loving cow keep all the plants watered? Look out for the scary fangflowers as they try to zap the cow. How long can you help it keep the garden happy?

What happens

When the game starts, a cow with a watering can appears in the garden, but there is only one flower. Every few seconds another flower appears or an existing flower begins to wilt. Use the arrow keys to move the cow to the wilted flowers and press the **Space bar** to water them. If any flower remains wilted for more than ten seconds, the game ends. But if the garden is happy for more than 15 seconds, one of the flowers mutates into a fangflower and tries to zap the cow.

◁ **Cow**
The cow is the main character in the game. Its aim is to keep all the flowers watered.

◁ **Fangflower**
This large carnivorous plant moves around the garden and tries to zap the cow.

The counter displays the number of seconds the garden has been happy for.

Pygame Zero Game

Garden happy for: 16 seconds

If a flower remains
wilted for more than ten
seconds, the game ends.

The blooming flowers
continue to appear at random
positions on the screen as
the game progresses.

◁ **Keep moo-ving!**
There are a lot of different
elements in this game. The
code uses several functions
to keep track of them all.

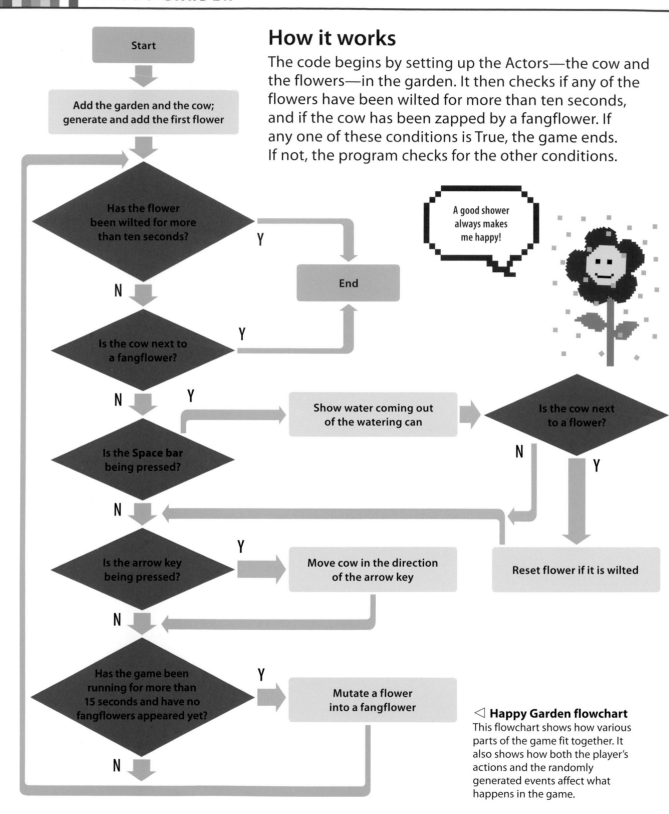

Start

Add the garden and the cow; generate and add the first flower

Has the flower been wilted for more than ten seconds?

Y → End

N

Is the cow next to a fangflower?

Y → End

N

Is the Space bar being pressed?

Y → Show water coming out of the watering can → Is the cow next to a flower?

N

Y → Reset flower if it is wilted

Is the arrow key being pressed?

Y → Move cow in the direction of the arrow key

N

Has the game been running for more than 15 seconds and have no fangflowers appeared yet?

Y → Mutate a flower into a fangflower

N

How it works

The code begins by setting up the Actors—the cow and the flowers—in the garden. It then checks if any of the flowers have been wilted for more than ten seconds, and if the cow has been zapped by a fangflower. If any one of these conditions is True, the game ends. If not, the program checks for the other conditions.

A good shower always makes me happy!

◁ **Happy Garden flowchart**
This flowchart shows how various parts of the game fit together. It also shows how both the player's actions and the randomly generated events affect what happens in the game.

It's gardening time!

It will take some preparation to get the garden ready. Begin by setting up the folders and downloading the images you'll need.

These are going to look great in my garden.

1 Get started

Open IDLE and create an empty file by clicking on the **File** menu and choosing **New File**.

File
New File
Open...
Open Module...
Recent Files ▶
Class Browser

2 Save the game

Go to your python-games folder and create another folder called *happy-garden*. From the **File** menu, choose **Save As...** and save the program as *garden.py* inside the happy-garden folder.

Save As:	garden.py
Tags:	
Where:	happy-garden

Cancel   Save

3 Set up an image folder

Within the happy-garden folder, create another folder by right-clicking and choosing **New Folder**. Name it *images*. It will be used to store all the images you need for this game.

happy-garden
garden.py
images

4 Put the images into the folder

Find the images for Happy Garden in the Python Games Resource Pack (**dk.com/computercoding**) and copy them into the images folder. Your folders should look like this now.

happy-garden
garden.py
images
cow-water.png
cow.png
fangflower.png
flower-wilt.png
flower.png
garden.png
zap.png

5 Import modules

It's time to start coding. Go back to your garden.py file and start by importing some modules. You'll use **randint()** to randomly choose which flowers will wilt or mutate. The functions in the Time module will keep track of how long the garden has been happy for or how long any flowers have been wilted.

```
from random import randint
import time
```

This imports Python's Time module.

This imports the **randint()** function from Python's Random module.

6 **Declare global variables**
Next define the global variables. These are the variables that will be used throughout the game. Type this code under the lines you added in Step 5.

```
WIDTH = 800
HEIGHT = 600
CENTER_X = WIDTH / 2
CENTER_Y = HEIGHT / 2

game_over = False
finalized = False
garden_happy = True
fangflower_collision = False

time_elapsed = 0
start_time = time.time()
```

These variables define the size of the game screen.

These are flag variables, which let you know what's happening in the game.

These variables help keep track of the time.

7 **Add the cow**
To start with, the only Actor in the game is the cow. Type the code shown in black to add the cow and set its starting position.

```
start_time = time.time()

cow = Actor("cow")
cow.pos = 100, 500
```

These values set the cow's starting position on the screen.

8 **Create lists for other Actors**
The other Actors in the game—flowers and fangflowers—are generated at random as the game progresses. Since you don't know how many of them will be generated, create lists to store each one that appears.

```
flower_list = []
wilted_list = []
fangflower_list = []
```

Each time a new flower Actor is created, it gets added to this list.

This list will store how long a flower has been wilted.

This list will store the fangflower Actors.

9 **Keep track of the fangflowers**
In this game, you need to pay special attention to the zapping fangflowers. You'll need to make them move around the garden. They also need to bounce off the edges of the game window so that they are always on the screen. You can do this by keeping track of their velocity—the speed at which something moves in a particular direction—along the x-axis and the y-axis. Add these lines after the code from Step 8.

```
fangflower_vy_list = []
fangflower_vx_list = []
```

This will hold the velocities of the fangflowers along the y-axis.

This will hold the velocities of the fangflowers along the x-axis.

10 **Draw the garden**
Now that you've set up those variables, you need to draw the garden and the cow. There are no flowers or fangflowers to draw yet, but add the code that will draw them when they're generated. Add these lines immediately after the code from Step 9.

This code draws the cow on the screen.

This code will draw all the flowers.

This will draw all the fangflowers.

This code checks how long the game has been running for.

```python
def draw():
    global game_over, time_elapsed, finalized
    if not game_over:
        screen.clear()
        screen.blit("garden", (0, 0))
        cow.draw()
        for flower in flower_list:
            flower.draw()
        for fangflower in fangflower_list:
            fangflower.draw()
        time_elapsed = int(time.time() - start_time)
        screen.draw.text(
            "Garden happy for: " +
            str(time_elapsed) + " seconds",
            topleft=(10, 10), color="black"
        )
```

11 **Time to test**
It's time to take a look at your garden! Save the IDLE file and then run it from the command line in the Command Prompt or Terminal window.

```
pgzrun
```

Type this in the Command Prompt or Terminal window and then drag and drop the garden.py file.

12 **Get a sneak peek!**
If there are no mistakes in your code, you should see a screen like this. If something's wrong, don't worry! Just use your debugging skills to check that you've spelled everything correctly and used the correct number of spaces for indentation.

You should see the garden and the cow holding a watering can.

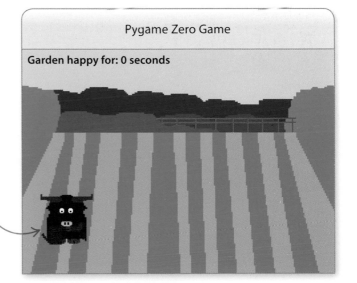

Pygame Zero Game

Garden happy for: 0 seconds

13 Other functions

You'll use a lot of functions in this game. You can list some of them now and define them later in the code. Using **pass** will make sure that Python doesn't run anything yet. Type this code under what you added in Step 10.

```python
def new_flower():
    pass

def add_flowers():
    pass

def check_wilt_times():
    pass

def wilt_flower():
    pass

def check_flower_collision():
    pass

def reset_cow():
    pass

def update():
    pass
```

Don't forget to save your work.

I'm going to make them all bloom.

14 Moving around the garden

At the moment, the cow appears on the screen but doesn't do anything. Add some code that lets you move the cow around. Replace the word **pass** under **def update()** with the following code.

This moves the cow five pixels to the right when the **Right** arrow key is pressed.

```python
def update():
    global score, game_over, fangflower_collision
    global flower_list, fangflower_list, time_elapsed
    if not game_over:
        if keyboard.left and cow.x > 0:
            cow.x -= 5
        elif keyboard.right and cow.x < WIDTH:
            cow.x += 5
        elif keyboard.up and cow.y > 150:
            cow.y -= 5
        elif keyboard.down and cow.y < HEIGHT:
            cow.y += 5
```

15 **Another test**
Test your newly updated code to make sure it's correct. Save your IDLE file and run it from the command line. You should now be able to move the cow on the screen.

Let's check pages 24–25 to see how it's done.

```
pgzrun
```

Type this in the Command Prompt or Terminal window and then drag and drop the garden.py file.

16 **Add a flower**
In this step, you'll create a flower Actor for the cow to water and add it to the end of **flower_list**. You'll also add the value **happy** to the end of **wilted_list**, which holds the amount of time each flower has been wilted for. The **happy** value will let the program know that the flower hasn't wilted. Replace **pass** in the **new_flower()** function with this code.

These are the global variables this function uses.

This line creates a new flower Actor.

```
def new_flower():
    global flower_list, wilted_list
    flower_new = Actor("flower")
    flower_new.pos = randint(50, WIDTH - 50), randint(150, HEIGHT - 100)
    flower_list.append(flower_new)
    wilted_list.append("happy")
    return
```

This line sets the position of the new flower.

This lets the program know that the flower is not wilted.

This adds the new flower to the list of flowers.

17 **Add more flowers to the garden**
Having just one flower to water would make the game too easy. You need to add some code that will create a new flower every four seconds to keep the cow busy. Add this code to replace the word **pass** under **def add_flowers()**.

```
def add_flowers():
    global game_over
    if not game_over:
        new_flower()
        clock.schedule(add_flowers, 4)
    return
```

I think I need a bigger garden!

This line calls the **new_flower()** function to create a new flower.

This adds a new flower every four seconds.

18 Start adding flowers
Although **add_flowers()** will schedule a call to itself every four seconds, you need to call it once in the program to start this process. Add the line in black above **def update()** from Step 13. Save and run your code to check if the flowers start appearing!

```
def reset_cow():
    pass


add_flowers()


def update():
```

19 Blooming garden
If there are no errors in your code, you will see a new flower appear on the screen every four seconds. This is what your screen will look like after 20 seconds. Use the arrow keys to move the cow around.

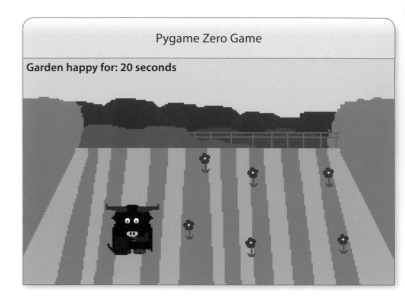

20 Water the flowers
It's time for the cow to water the wilted flowers. Let's add some code that will make the cow sprinkle water on the flowers when the player presses the **Space bar**. The code will also check if the cow is standing next to a flower. Add this code to the **update()** function.

```
    global flower_list, fangflower_list, time_elapsed
    if not game_over:
        if keyboard.space:
            cow.image = "cow-water"
            clock.schedule(reset_cow, 0.5)
            check_flower_collision()
        if keyboard.left and cow.x > 0:
            cow.x -= 5
```

This will check if the **Space bar** is being pressed.

This will change the image of the cow to the one with water coming out of the watering can.

This will reset the cow's image after half a second.

This line will check if the cow is next to a flower.

21 Stop watering

The code from Step 20 uses two functions that you haven't written yet—**reset_cow()** and **check_flower_collision()**. Let's add the code that will change the image of the cow using the watering can back to the version where it's just holding it. Replace the word **pass** under the **reset_cow()** function from Step 13 with the code in black below.

```
def reset_cow():
    global game_over
    if not game_over:
        cow.image = "cow"
    return


add_flowers()
```

This code runs if the game is not over yet.

This changes the cow's image back to the original one.

Uhh... I think that's enough water.

22 Points for accuracy!

You need the code to check if the cow is near a flower when the **Space bar** is pressed. If it is, the flower will get watered and its "time since flower wilted" value in **wilted_list** will be set to **happy**. To do this, you'll use Pygame Zero's built-in **colliderect()** function to check if a flower and the cow have collided or are next to each other. Replace **pass** under **def check_flower_collision()** in Step 13 with the code shown below.

```
def check_flower_collision():
    global cow, flower_list, wilted_list
    index = 0
    for flower in flower_list:
        if (flower.colliderect(cow) and
                flower.image == "flower-wilt"):
            flower.image = "flower"
            wilted_list[index] = "happy"
            break
        index = index + 1
    return
```

These are the global variables you will use in this function.

This code loops through all the flowers in the list.

This variable helps the program to move through the list in order.

This condition applies if the cow is next to the flower you're looking at.

This changes the wilted flower's image back to the original version.

This line updates the value of **index** so that the program moves through the list.

This stops the loop from checking the other flowers.

This line stops the program counting how long the flower's been wilted.

23   Wilt a flower

It's time to give your garden-tending cow a bit of a challenge. Add some code that will wilt a random flower every three seconds. The cow will have to dash to the wilted flower to water it. Replace the word **pass** in the **wilt_flower()** function from Step 13 with the code below.

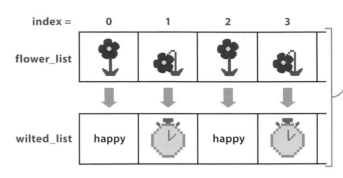

index = 0 1 2 3

flower_list

wilted_list   happy   happy

These two lists store the information of a particular flower at the same index number.

```python
def wilt_flower():
    global flower_list, wilted_list, game_over
    if not game_over:
        if flower_list:
            rand_flower = randint(0, len(flower_list) - 1)
            if (flower_list[rand_flower].image == "flower"):
                flower_list[rand_flower].image = "flower-wilt"
                wilted_list[rand_flower] = time.time()
    clock.schedule(wilt_flower, 3)
    return
```

This line resets the time for this flower in **wilted_list** to the current time.

This schedules another call to **wilt_flower()** in three seconds.

This line generates a random index in the list of flowers.

This checks if the flower at this index is wilted or not.

This sets the flower image to a wilted flower image.

24   Unhappy garden!

Next you need to check if any of the flowers have been wilted for more than ten seconds. If one has, the garden's unhappy, and it's game over! Go to **def check_wilt_times()** in Step 13 and replace **pass** with the code shown here.

This code loops over each item in the **wilted_list**.

```python
def check_wilt_times():
    global wilted_list, game_over, garden_happy
    if wilted_list:
        for wilted_since in wilted_list:
            if (not wilted_since == "happy"):
                time_wilted = int(time.time() - wilted_since)
                if (time_wilted) > 10.0:
                    garden_happy = False
                    game_over = True
                    break
    return
```

This checks if there are any items in the **wilted_list**.

This line checks if the flower has been wilted for more than ten seconds.

These lines check if the flower is wilted and work out how long it's been wilted.

25 **Start wilting**
Now that you've added a function to wilt the flowers, you need to call it. Add this code just below the call to **add_flowers()** that you added in Step 18.

```
              cow.image="cow"
    return

add_flowers()
wilt_flower()
```

This command will make the flowers wilt.

26 **Check for happiness**
Now you need to add a call to the **check_wilt_times()** function you defined in Step 24. Go to the **update()** function and add this line.

```
def update():
    global score, game_over, fangflower_collision
    global flower_list, fangflower_list, time_elapsed
    check_wilt_times()
    if not game_over:
```

This checks how long the flowers have been wilted.

27 **Game over!**
Your game is almost ready! But before testing it, you need to add some code that lets the player know that the game is over if the flowers have been wilted for too long. Add an **else** branch to the **if not game_over** statement in the **draw()** function you defined in Step 10.

This line displays a message to show how long the garden has been happy.

```
            str(time_elapsed) + " seconds",
            topleft=(10, 10), color="black"
        )
    else:
        if not finalized:
            cow.draw()
            screen.draw.text(
                "Garden happy for: " +
                str(time_elapsed) + " seconds",
                topleft=(10, 10), color="black"
            )
            if (not garden_happy):
                screen.draw.text(
                    "GARDEN UNHAPPY—GAME OVER!", color="black",
                    topleft=(10, 50)
                )
            finalized = True
```

This displays a message that tells the player the game is over.

28 Test run
Save your IDLE file and run it from the command line in the Command Prompt or Terminal window. Try moving the cow around and water the wilted flowers. If a flower remains wilted for more than ten seconds, you will see a screen like the one shown here.

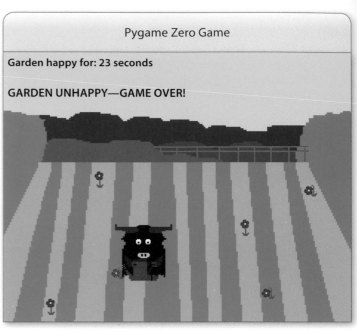

Pygame Zero Game

Garden happy for: 23 seconds

GARDEN UNHAPPY—GAME OVER!

Code testing makes me really giddy!

29 Added menace
So far, keeping the garden happy has been difficult but not dangerous. What if the flowers start mutating into scary fangflowers that move around the garden trying to zap the cow? Let's add some functions to control the fangflower. Use placeholders for now and define them later on. Type this code above the **reset_cow()** function you defined in Step 21.

Where did these weird flowers come from?

```
        index = index + 1
    return


def check_fangflower_collision():
    pass


def velocity():
    pass


def mutate():
    pass


def update_fangflowers():
    pass


def reset_cow():
    global game_over
    if not game_over:
        cow.image = "cow"
```

30 Mutation

It's time for your harmless flowers to turn into carnivorous fangflowers. Even worse, the code will change one random flower into a fangflower every 20 seconds after the first mutation. Replace **pass** under **def mutate()** with the code below. There's a lot of code to add here, so be extra careful.

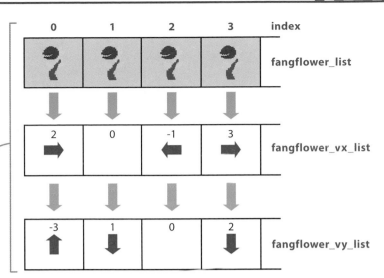

These three lists will store the velocities of a particular fangflower at the same index number.

If the game is not over and there are still flowers left to mutate, this block of code will run.

These are the global variables needed in this function.

```
def mutate():
    global flower_list, fangflower_list, fangflower_vy_list
    global fangflower_vx_list, game_over
    if not game_over and flower_list:
        rand_flower = randint(0, len(flower_list) - 1)
        fangflower_pos_x = flower_list[rand_flower].x
        fangflower_pos_y = flower_list[rand_flower].y
        del flower_list[rand_flower]
        fangflower = Actor("fangflower")
        fangflower.pos = fangflower_pos_x, fangflower_pos_y
        fangflower_vx = velocity()
        fangflower_vy = velocity()
        fangflower = fangflower_list.append(fangflower)
        fangflower_vx_list.append(fangflower_vx)
        fangflower_vy_list.append(fangflower_vy)
        clock.schedule(mutate, 20)
    return
```

This line picks a random flower to mutate.

This line removes the mutated flower from the list of flowers.

This line sets the fangflower at the same position as the flower it mutated from.

This sets how fast the fangflower is moving left or right on the screen.

This sets how fast the fangflower is moving up or down on the screen.

This adds a new fangflower to the list of fangflowers.

The fangflower's velocities are added to these lists.

This line schedules a call to mutate a flower every 20 seconds.

31 Move the fangflower

Unlike other flowers, the fangflowers don't stay in one place. They move all over the garden trying to zap the cow. In this step, you'll add the code that generates the velocity of each fangflower along the x-axis and y-axis. The fangflowers will use a combination of these two velocities to move up, down, side to side, or diagonally. Add the following code under **def velocity()** from Step 29.

Remember, we talked about velocity on page 160.

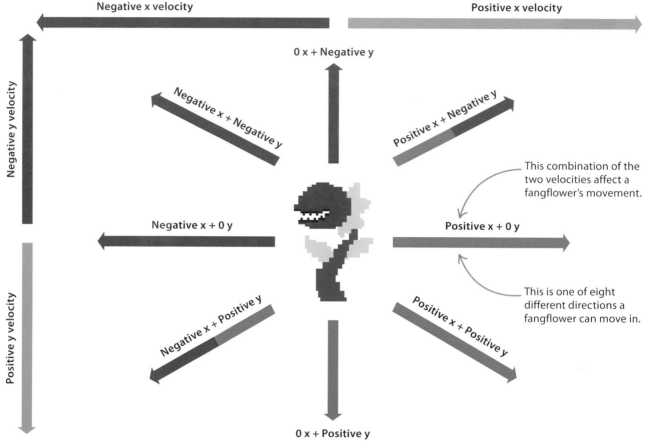

Negative x velocity

Positive x velocity

0 x + Negative y

Negative x + Negative y

Positive x + Negative y

Negative y velocity

This combination of the two velocities affect a fangflower's movement.

Negative x + 0 y

Positive x + 0 y

This is one of eight different directions a fangflower can move in.

Positive y velocity

Negative x + Positive y

Positive x + Positive y

0 x + Positive y

This generates the velocity of the fangflower with no direction yet.

This line generates a number that represents the direction of the fangflower.

If the direction is **0**, this returns a negative velocity.

If the direction is **1**, this returns a positive velocity.

```
def velocity():
    random_dir = randint(0, 1)
    random_velocity = randint(2, 3)
    if random_dir == 0:
        return -random_velocity
    else:
        return random_velocity
```

32 Update the fangflowers

It's time for the fangflowers to start moving. The code in this step will be called every time the **update()** function runs. It will also keep the fangflowers inside the garden by making them bounce off the edges of the game screen. Replace **pass** under **def update_fangflowers()** from Step 29 with this code. There's a lot of tricky code here, so type it in carefully.

These are the global variables used in this function.

```
def update_fangflowers():
    global fangflower_list, game_over
    if not game_over:
        index = 0
        for fangflower in fangflower_list:
            fangflower_vx = fangflower_vx_list[index]
            fangflower_vy = fangflower_vy_list[index]
            fangflower.x = fangflower.x + fangflower_vx
            fangflower.y = fangflower.y + fangflower_vy
            if fangflower.left < 0:
                fangflower_vx_list[index] = -fangflower_vx
            if fangflower.right > WIDTH:
                fangflower_vx_list[index] = -fangflower_vx
            if fangflower.top < 150:
                fangflower_vy_list[index] = -fangflower_vy
            if fangflower.bottom > HEIGHT:
                fangflower_vy_list[index] = -fangflower_vy
            index = index + 1
    return
```

This variable helps the program keep track of which item in the list it's dealing with.

This loops over all the fangflowers in the list.

These get the x and y velocities of the fangflower.

These get the new position of the fangflower.

If the fangflower touches the left edge of the screen, this will make it start moving to the right.

By changing its y velocity, the fangflower is brought back into the screen.

Better make sure none of you wander off!

33 **Check for collisions**

Now that your fangflowers are in motion, you need to add some code that will check if a fangflower has caught up with the cow to zap it! Replace **pass** in the **check_fangflower_collision()** function with the code shown below.

These are the global variables used in this function.

This adds an image to show the cow has been zapped.

This tells the program that the game is over.

```
def check_fangflower_collision():
    global cow, fangflower_list, fangflower_collision
    global game_over
    for fangflower in fangflower_list:
        if fangflower.colliderect(cow):
            cow.image = "zap"
            game_over = True
            break
    return
```

This checks if the fangflower and cow are next to each other.

This line stops the program from checking other fangflowers.

34 **Drawing results**

If a fangflower manages to zap the cow, it's game over. Add this code to the **draw()** function to display a game over message.

Don't forget to save your work.

This block of code runs if the garden is still happy but the cow has been zapped.

This draws a message on the screen to show the game is over because of a fangflower attack.

This makes sure the code is not run again.

```
    if (not garden_happy):
        screen.draw.text(
            "GARDEN UNHAPPY—GAME OVER!", color="black",
            topleft=(10, 100)
        )
        finalized = True
    else:
        screen.draw.text(
            "FANGFLOWER ATTACK—GAME OVER!", color="black",
            topleft=(10, 50)
        )
        finalized = True
    return
```

35 **Set up the update**

The fangflowers are ready to attack. The last thing you need to do is add some code that starts the whole mutation process if the garden has been happy for more than 15 seconds. Go to the **update()** function and add the code as shown here.

```
def update():
    global score, game_over, fangflower_collision
    global flower_list, fangflower_list, time_elapsed
    fangflower_collision = check_fangflower_collision()
    check_wilt_times()
    if not game_over:
        if keyboard.space:
            cow.image = "cow-water"
            clock.schedule(reset_cow, 0.5)
            check_flower_collision()
        if keyboard.left and cow.x > 0:
            cow.x -= 5
        elif keyboard.right and cow.x < WIDTH:
            cow.x += 5
        elif keyboard.up and cow.y > 150:
            cow.y -= 5
        elif keyboard.down and cow.y < HEIGHT:
            cow.y += 5
        if time_elapsed > 15 and not fangflower_list:
            mutate()
        update_fangflowers()
```

This checks if the garden has been happy for more than 15 seconds and if any fangflowers have appeared on the screen yet.

This line mutates a flower into a fangflower.

36 **Test and play!**

Green thumbs at the ready, your game can now be played! Save and run the file from the command line. Make sure the cow keeps the flowers watered while avoiding the dangerous fangflowers. What does your screen look like when the fangflowers appear and finally zap the cow?

We've run all the tests. You're good to go!

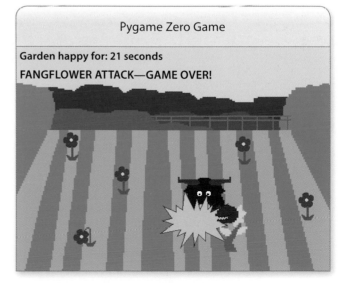

Pygame Zero Game

Garden happy for: 21 seconds
FANGFLOWER ATTACK—GAME OVER!

Hacks and tweaks

Do you want to make the game even more exciting? You can try out some of these ideas and add new features to the game.

```
random_velocity = randint(2, 3)
```

△ **Faster fangflowers!**
You can make the fangflowers move faster by changing the possible range of **random_velocity**. Try increasing the range by using something like **randint(4, 6)**.

Sorry pal, your day in the sun is over.

△ **Change the gardener**
You might think a cow is an unusual gardener. Why don't you look for another character in the Python Game Resource Pack? You could also make a new character using any 8-bit editor available online.

```
clock.schedule(add_flowers, 4)
```

△ **More flowers**
You can change how often a new flower appears on the screen to make the game easier or harder. Update the code under **def add_flowers()** to change how often it schedules a call to itself.

```
clock.schedule(mutate, 20)
```

△ **More fangflowers**
Is the game too hard or too easy? You can change the code in **mutate()** to make fangflowers appear more or less often.

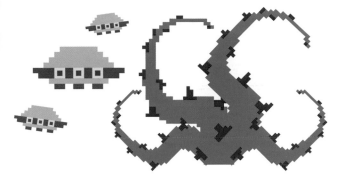

◁ Add new enemies

If you find the game is not challenging enough at the moment, you can add more enemies. Use an online 8-bit editor to create more characters and then add some functions to control their behavior. These functions would be similar to the ones that control the fangflowers in the game. The new enemies could be flowers that fire pellets at the cow if it gets too close, thorn bushes that snake out long stems to catch the cow, or even aliens in flying saucers who are after the fangflowers.

△ Rain in the garden

What happens if it rains in the garden? The flowers will be much happier and wouldn't need watering. But they will also mutate into fangflowers more quickly. To make it look like it's raining, you can update the background with another image from the Python Games Resource Pack or create a new background on your own. To control the new background, create a new variable called **raining** and change the **draw()** function to update the background based on the variable's value.

```
if not raining:
    screen.blit("garden", (0, 0))
else:
    screen.blit("garden-raining", (0, 0))
```

Sleeping Dragons

How to build Sleeping Dragons

Grab your shield and sword as you go in search of dragon treasure. Time your movements to snatch the eggs from under the dragons' noses. But be careful, brave knight—if they wake up, you're in for a nasty surprise!

What happens

In this game, the player controls the hero using the four arrow keys. The hero must collect 20 eggs from the dragons' lair to win the game. Each dragon sleeps and wakes up at different times. If the hero is near a dragon when it's awake, the player loses a life. The game ends when the player runs out of lives or collects enough eggs.

◁ **Dragons**
The three dragons are harmless when they're asleep.

◁ **Eggs**
Each dragon has a different number of eggs.

◁ **Hero**
The fearless hero has three lives to collect 20 eggs.

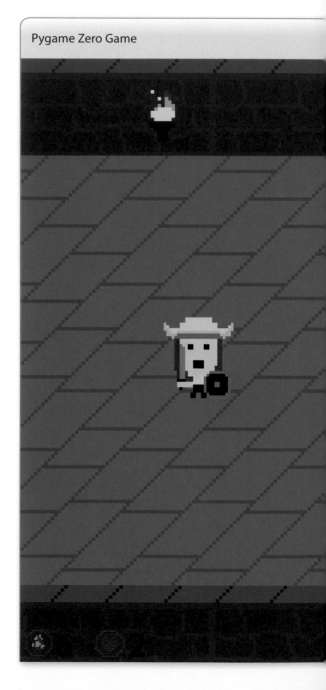

Pygame Zero Game

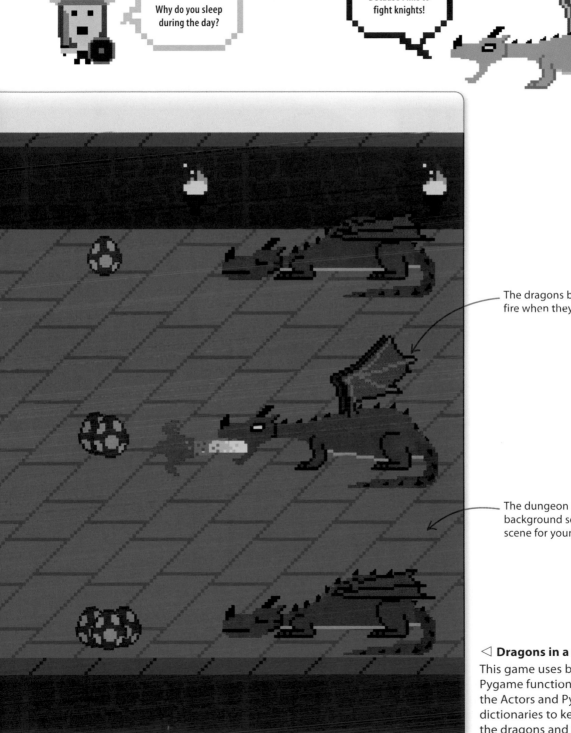

The dragons breathe fire when they wake up.

The dungeon background sets the scene for your quest.

◁ **Dragons in a dungeon**
This game uses built-in Pygame functions to animate the Actors and Python's dictionaries to keep track of the dragons and their eggs.

How it works

You'll use the **draw()** function to draw the hero, the dragons, and the eggs on the screen. Then you'll create the **update()** function to check the player's actions and update the different elements of the game. Both these functions are called many times every second, which will allow you to animate the Actors in the game. You'll also use the **clock.schedule_interval()** function to wake up the dragons and send them to sleep at regular intervals.

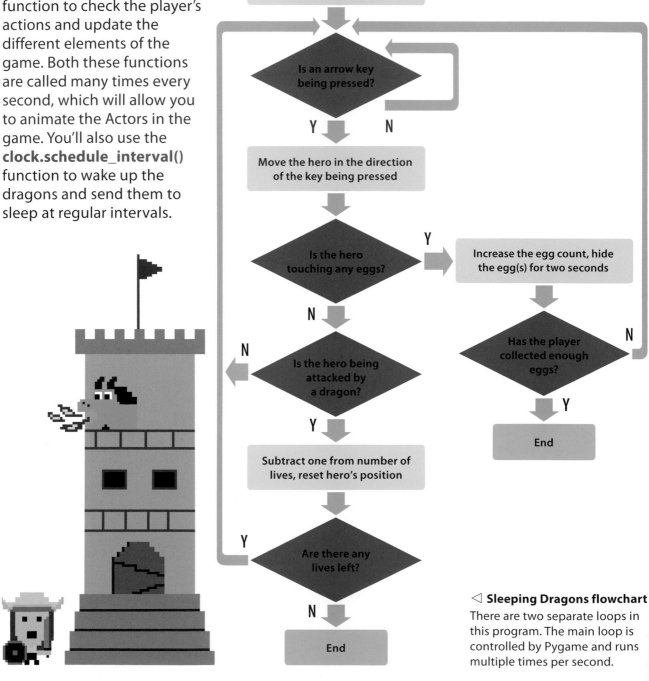

◁ **Sleeping Dragons flowchart**
There are two separate loops in this program. The main loop is controlled by Pygame and runs multiple times per second.

▷ **Dragon animation flowchart**
The second loop in the program is responsible for the dragons' sleep cycle. It runs once every second.

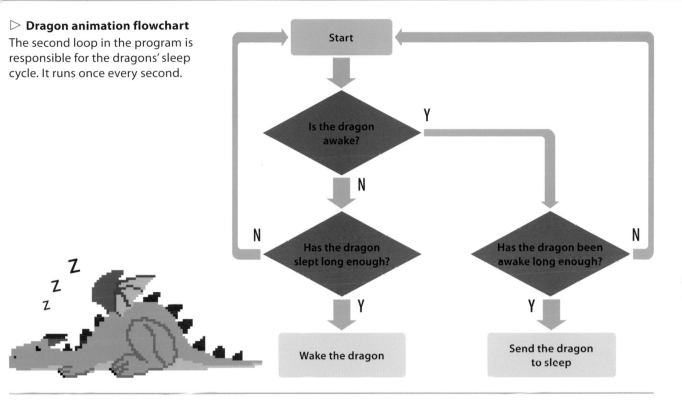

Begin the quest

First you'll create the variables that will track the game's progress. Then you'll write some code that will draw all the elements on the screen. Finally, you'll set up the functions to make the hero move, handle the dragons' sleep cycles, and check if the hero has collected enough eggs without getting caught.

I need some more eggs!

1 **Time to begin**
Open IDLE and create an empty file by going to the **File** menu and selecting **New File**.

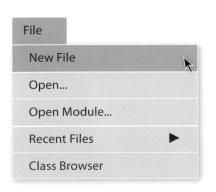

2 Save the file

Go to your python-games folder and create another folder, called *sleeping-dragons*, inside it. Then go to the **File** menu and select **Save As...** to save the IDLE file as *dragons.py* in this folder.

Save As:	dragons.py
Tags:	
Where:	🗀 sleeping-dragons

Cancel   Save

I name thee Margaret.

?

3 Add the images

This game uses nine images. Create a new folder, called *images*, inside the sleeping-dragons folder. Find all the images in the Python Games Resource Pack (**dk.com/computercoding**) and copy them into this folder.

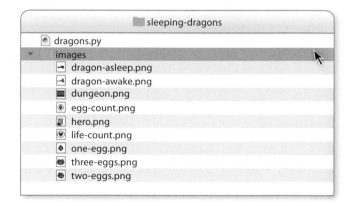

🗀 sleeping-dragons
- 📄 dragons.py
- 📁 images
  - 🖼 dragon-asleep.png
  - 🖼 dragon-awake.png
  - 🖼 dungeon.png
  - 🖼 egg-count.png
  - 🖼 hero.png
  - 🖼 life-count.png
  - 🖼 one-egg.png
  - 🖼 three-eggs.png
  - 🖼 two-eggs.png

4 Import a module

Now you can start writing the code. Begin by importing Python's Math module. Type this at the very top of your IDLE file.

```
import math
```

This imports the entire module.

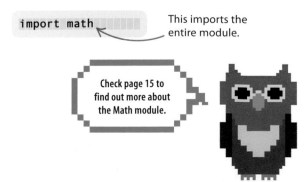

Check page 15 to find out more about the Math module.

5 Declare the constants

You need to declare the constants at the start of the game. In this game, you'll use constants to determine many things, including the hero's starting position and the number of eggs the player needs to collect to win the game. All of these constants will be used later in the code. Type this under the line from Step 4.

Don't forget to save your work.

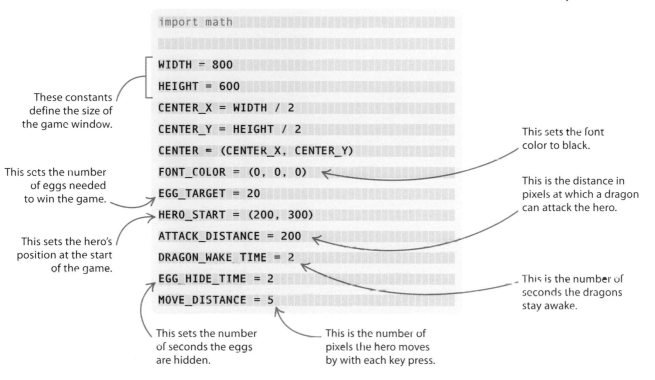

These constants define the size of the game window.

This sets the number of eggs needed to win the game.

This sets the hero's position at the start of the game.

This sets the font color to black.

This is the distance in pixels at which a dragon can attack the hero.

This is the number of seconds the dragons stay awake.

This sets the number of seconds the eggs are hidden.

This is the number of pixels the hero moves by with each key press.

```
import math

WIDTH = 800
HEIGHT = 600
CENTER_X = WIDTH / 2
CENTER_Y = HEIGHT / 2
CENTER = (CENTER_X, CENTER_Y)
FONT_COLOR = (0, 0, 0)
EGG_TARGET = 20
HERO_START = (200, 300)
ATTACK_DISTANCE = 200
DRAGON_WAKE_TIME = 2
EGG_HIDE_TIME = 2
MOVE_DISTANCE = 5
```

6 Declare the global variables

After the constants, you need to declare the global variables. They're a lot like constants because they're usually declared at the top of the program. However, unlike constants, their values change when they're used throughout the program to track the game's progress. Type this code next.

Check page 74 to learn more about global variables.

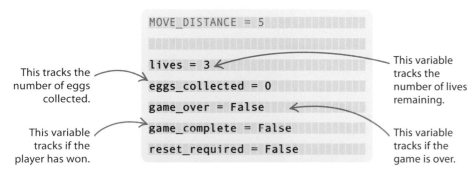

This tracks the number of eggs collected.

This variable tracks if the player has won.

This variable tracks the number of lives remaining.

This variable tracks if the game is over.

```
MOVE_DISTANCE = 5

lives = 3
eggs_collected = 0
game_over = False
game_complete = False
reset_required = False
```

7 Create the lairs

Each dragon in this game has its own lair with a certain number of eggs and an easy, medium, or hard difficulty level. You can use Python's dictionaries to keep track of all the elements needed to create these lairs. Each dictionary includes Actors for the dragons and eggs, and variables for tracking each dragon's sleep cycle. Begin by creating a dictionary for the easiest lair. Carefully type these lines under the code from Step 6.

```python
reset_required = False

easy_lair = {
    "dragon": Actor("dragon-asleep", pos=(600, 100)),
    "eggs": Actor("one-egg", pos=(400, 100)),
    "egg_count": 1,
    "egg_hidden": False,
    "egg_hide_counter": 0,
    "sleep_length": 10,
    "sleep_counter": 0,
    "wake_counter": 0
}
```

EXPERT TIPS

Dictionaries

In Python, using a dictionary is another way to store information. It's like a list, but with a label attached to every item. This label is known as the "key" and the item it's attached to is called the "value." You can even create a dictionary in which the values are other dictionaries. This is called "nesting," and it allows you to store the pieces of your game in a structured way.

cherries   clock

paint bucket   trophy

8 Medium lair

Next add a dictionary for the lair with medium difficulty. The code for this is a lot like the code in the previous step, but some of the values are different.

These are the coordinates for the dragon in this lair.

```python
}

medium_lair = {
    "dragon": Actor("dragon-asleep", pos=(600, 300)),
    "eggs": Actor("two-eggs", pos=(400, 300)),
    "egg_count": 2,
    "egg_hidden": False,
    "egg_hide_counter": 0,
    "sleep_length": 7,
    "sleep_counter": 0,
    "wake_counter": 0
}
```

This checks if the eggs are currently hidden.

This sets the coordinates of the eggs.

This tracks the dragon's sleep cycle.

9 Hard lair

Now you need to add the third and final lair. Add this code after what you typed in Step 8.

```
    "sleep_length": 7,
    "sleep_counter": 0,
    "wake_counter": 0
}

hard_lair = {
    "dragon": Actor("dragon-asleep", pos=(600, 500)),
    "eggs": Actor("three-eggs", pos=(400, 500)),
    "egg_count": 3,
    "egg_hidden": False,
    "egg_hide_counter": 0,
    "sleep_length": 4,
    "sleep_counter": 0,
    "wake_counter": 0
}
```

This is just too hard!

This sets the numbers of eggs for this lair.

This tracks how many seconds the eggs have been hidden for.

10 Bring the lairs together

You'll need to loop over all the lairs later on in the code. To make this easier, store them in a list. Type this line next.

```
    "sleep_counter": 0,
    "wake_counter": 0
}

lairs = [easy_lair, medium_lair, hard_lair]
```

This list holds all the lairs.

11 A hero is born

The final Actor needed for this game is the hero. It's the character that the player controls to collect the dragon eggs.

```
lairs = [easy_lair, medium_lair, hard_lair]
hero = Actor("hero", pos=HERO_START)
```

This sets the starting position of the hero Actor.

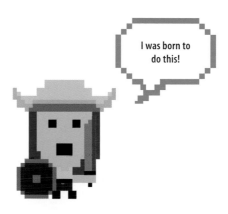

I was born to do this!

12 Draw the Actors

Now use the **draw()** function to display all the Actors on the screen. Add the following code under the lines you typed in Step 11. There's quite a bit to add here, so be careful.

One down, two to go!

```python
hero = Actor("hero", pos=HERO_START)

def draw():
    global lairs, eggs_collected, lives, game_complete
    screen.clear()
    screen.blit("dungeon", (0, 0))
    if game_over:
        screen.draw.text("GAME OVER!", fontsize=60, center=CENTER, color=FONT_COLOR)
    elif game_complete:
        screen.draw.text("YOU WON!", fontsize=60, center=CENTER, color=FONT_COLOR)
    else:
        hero.draw()
        draw_lairs(lairs)
        draw_counters(eggs_collected, lives)
```

This adds a background to the game.

13 Create the stubs

Next create the placeholders for some functions that will be defined later on. Using **pass** will tell Python not to run these functions yet. Type this code below the lines from Step 12.

```python
def draw_lairs(lairs_to_draw):
    pass

def draw_counters(eggs_collected, lives):
    pass
```

14 Run the code

Save your file and run it from the command line. Check pages 24–25 if you need to remind yourself how to do this.

```
pgzrun
```

Type this command in the Command Prompt or Terminal window, then drag the dragons.py file here to run it.

Enter the dungeon

If your code is free of errors, you'll see a screen similar to the one shown here. You'll see the hero and the dungeon, but you won't be able to move the hero around yet. The dragons and eggs will be added in the next step.

The hero appears at the starting position.

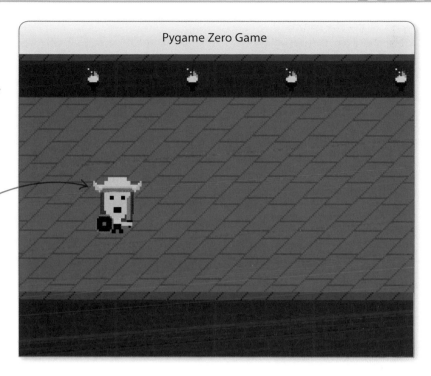

Pygame Zero Game

Draw the lairs

You now need to define the **draw_lairs()** function. It takes a parameter called **lairs_to_draw**. This function loops over the three lairs—**easy_lair**, **medium_lair**, **hard_lair**—and draws a dragon for each of them. If the eggs are not currently hidden, they are drawn as well. To get the Actors from the dictionaries of all the lairs, type the name of the dictionary followed by the key in square brackets. Replace **pass** under **draw_lairs(lairs_to_draw)** from Step 13 with this code.

Don't forget to save your work.

```
    else:
        hero.draw()
        draw_lairs(lairs)
        draw_counters(eggs_collected, lives)

def draw_lairs(lairs_to_draw):
    for lair in lairs_to_draw:
        lair["dragon"].draw()
        if lair["egg_hidden"] is False:
            lair["eggs"].draw()
```

This draws a dragon Actor for each lair.

This draws the eggs for each lair if they are not currently hidden.

This loops over each lair.

17 Draw the counters

Next you'll define the **draw_counters()** function. It takes two parameters—**eggs_collected** and **lives**. Their values will be displayed in the bottom-left corner of the game screen. Replace **pass** under **def draw_counters(eggs_collected, lives)** with the code shown below.

That's enough eggs for one day.

```
def draw_counters(eggs_collected, lives):
    screen.blit("egg-count", (0, HEIGHT - 30))
    screen.draw.text(str(eggs_collected),
                     fontsize=40,
                     pos=(30, HEIGHT - 30),
                     color=FONT_COLOR)
    screen.blit("life-count", (60, HEIGHT - 30))
    screen.draw.text(str(lives),
                     fontsize=40,
                     pos=(90, HEIGHT - 30),
                     color=FONT_COLOR)
```

This draws an icon to represent the number of eggs collected.

This draws an icon to represent the number of lives the player has left.

18 Move the hero

With everything set up, it's time to add some code that will make the hero move on the screen. You'll use the **update()** function to do this. If the player presses an arrow key, this code will make the hero move in that direction by the number of pixels assigned to **MOVE_DISTANCE**. You also need to add a call to the **check_for_collisions()** function, which you'll define later. Type this code after the lines from Step 17.

```
def update():
    if keyboard.right:
        hero.x += MOVE_DISTANCE
        if hero.x > WIDTH:
            hero.x = WIDTH
    elif keyboard.left:
        hero.x -= MOVE_DISTANCE
        if hero.x < 0:
            hero.x = 0
    elif keyboard.down:
        hero.y += MOVE_DISTANCE
        if hero.y > HEIGHT:
            hero.y = HEIGHT
    elif keyboard.up:
        hero.y -= MOVE_DISTANCE
        if hero.y < 0:
            hero.y = 0
    check_for_collisions()
```

Hey, move! That's my spot.

19 Add a placeholder

This is a good point to run your game and check for any bugs. But before you run it, you need to set up a placeholder for the **check_for_collisions()** function. Add these lines after the code from Step 18.

```
check_for_collisions()

def check_for_collisions():
    pass
```

20 Try it out

Save your IDLE file and run it from the command line. If there are no bugs hiding in your code, you'll see a screen like the one below. You'll be able to make the hero move around the screen, but you won't be able to collect any eggs yet.

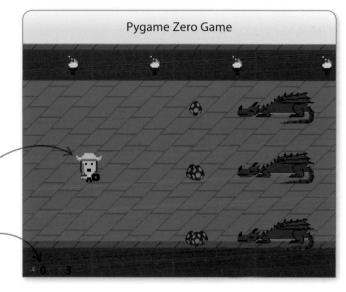

Pygame Zero Game

The hero moves in the direction of the arrow key being pressed.

The counters for the eggs collected and lives remaining appear in the bottom-left corner.

21 Animate the lairs

Now animate the dragons and the eggs to make the game more interesting. The **update_lairs()** function will loop through each lair dictionary and check if the dragon is asleep or awake. Add this code between the **update()** function and the **def check_for_collisions()** placeholder.

```
check_for_collisions()

def update_lairs():
    global lairs, hero, lives
    for lair in lairs:
        if lair["dragon"].image == "dragon-asleep":
            update_sleeping_dragon(lair)
        elif lair["dragon"].image == "dragon-awake":
            update_waking_dragon(lair)
        update_egg(lair)

def check_for_collisions():
```

This loops through all three lairs.

This block will animate the dragon.

This will animate the eggs.

This is called if the dragon is asleep.

This is called if the dragon is awake.

22 Schedule a call

Next add some code to schedule a call to the **update_lairs()** function once every second. Add this line under the code from Step 21.

```
update_egg(lair)

clock.schedule_interval(update_lairs, 1)
```

This function schedules a call to another function at regular intervals.

The number of seconds between each function call can be changed by updating this number.

23 Wake the sleeping dragon

Now you need to check if the dragon has slept long enough. To do this, you need to compare the **sleep_counter** with the **sleep_length** set for that dragon. If it's time to wake the dragon, the sleeping dragon image will be updated and the **sleep_counter** will be reset to **0**. If not, the **sleep_counter** will be increased by one. Add this code under the line from Step 22.

```
def update_sleeping_dragon(lair):
    if lair["sleep_counter"] >= lair["sleep_length"]:
        lair["dragon"].image = "dragon-awake"
        lair["sleep_counter"] = 0
    else:
        lair["sleep_counter"] += 1
```

This checks if the **sleep_counter** is greater than or equal to the **sleep_length** set for the dragon.

This resets the dragon's **sleep_counter** to **0**.

This increases the **sleep_counter** by one.

24 Send the dragon to sleep

If the dragon has been awake for long enough, it needs to be sent back to sleep. The function needed to do this is similar to the one you defined in the previous step. However, unlike **sleep_length**, which is different for all the dragons, the time they should be awake for is the same, so you'll use the constant **DRAGON_WAKE_TIME**. Add this code under what you typed in Step 23.

```
def update_waking_dragon(lair):
    if lair["wake_counter"] >= DRAGON_WAKE_TIME:
        lair["dragon"].image = "dragon-asleep"
        lair["wake_counter"] = 0
    else:
        lair["wake_counter"] += 1
```

This checks if the dragon has been awake long enough.

This resets the dragon's **wake_counter** to **0**.

This updates the dragon image.

This adds one to the **wake_counter**.

25 Animate the eggs

The program hides the eggs when the hero collects them. You need to check if the eggs have been hidden for long enough and, therefore, need to reappear. Add this code immediately after the lines from Step 24.

```
        lair["wake_counter"] += 1

def update_egg(lair):
    if lair["egg_hidden"] is True:
        if lair["egg_hide_counter"] >= EGG_HIDE_TIME:
            lair["egg_hidden"] = False
            lair["egg_hide_counter"] = 0
        else:
            lair["egg_hide_counter"] += 1
```

This function checks if any eggs need to stay hidden or not.

This block runs if any eggs have been hidden for long enough.

This adds one to the **egg_hide_counter**.

26 Test the code

Save your file and run it from the command line. You should see the dragons sleeping and waking up. Next you'll add the code that'll make the eggs disappear when the hero collects them.

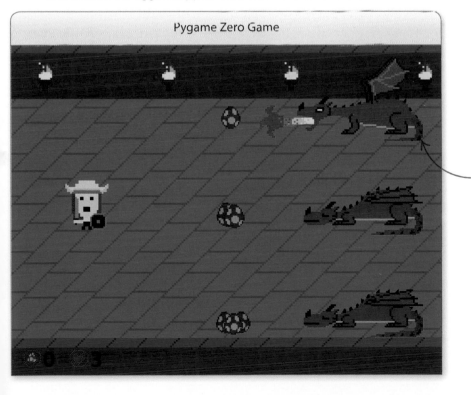

Pygame Zero Game

The dragons will wake up at different times.

27 Check for collisions

You now need to define the **check_for_collisions()** function from Step 19. The code in this function will loop over each lair dictionary and check if the hero has touched an egg and if the hero is close enough to an awake dragon to get attacked. Replace **pass** under **def_check_for_collisions()** with the code shown below.

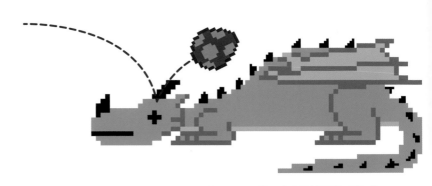

```
            lair["egg_hide_counter"] += 1


def check_for_collisions():
    global lairs, eggs_collected, lives, reset_required, game_complete
    for lair in lairs:
        if lair["egg_hidden"] is False:
            check_for_egg_collision(lair)
        if lair["dragon"].image == "dragon-awake" and reset_required is False:
            check_for_dragon_collision(lair)
```

This function is called if the eggs are not hidden.

This function is called if the dragon is awake and the hero's position is not being reset.

This makes sure the player doesn't lose a life when the hero is being moved back to the start position.

EXPERT TIPS

colliderect()

The **colliderect()** function gets its name from a combination of two words—collide and rectangle. Pygame places an invisible rectangle around each element on the screen. If you want to detect a collision between two objects, you can check if the rectangles around them are overlapping with each other. Sometimes Pygame detects a collision even if two objects appear to be slightly apart. This is because even when the objects are not touching each other, the rectangles around them can still overlap.

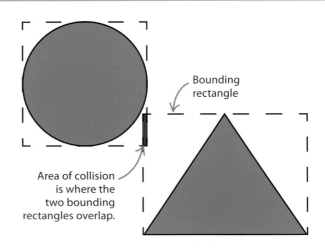

Bounding rectangle

Area of collision is where the two bounding rectangles overlap.

28 **Dragon collisions**

If the hero gets too close to an awake dragon, the player will lose a life. You'll use the **check_for_dragon_collision()** function to calculate this distance. Add this code under what you typed in Step 27.

Don't forget to save your work.

```
          check_for_dragon_collision(lair)


def check_for_dragon_collision(lair):
    x_distance = hero.x - lair["dragon"].x
    y_distance = hero.y - lair["dragon"].y
    distance = math.hypot(x_distance, y_distance)
    if distance < ATTACK_DISTANCE:
        handle_dragon_collision()
```

This calculates the horizontal and vertical distances between the dragon and the hero.

This finds the distance between the dragon and the hero in a straight line.

This function is called if the distance between the hero and dragon is less than **ATTACK_DISTANCE**.

29 **Reset hero**

If the player loses a life, the hero's position needs to be reset to the starting position. You'll use the **animate()** function to do this. In your game, this function takes three parameters—the hero Actor, the hero's starting position, and the **subtract_life()** function. Add the code shown in black here.

```
    distance = math.hypot(x_distance, y_distance)
    if distance < ATTACK_DISTANCE:
        handle_dragon_collision()


def handle_dragon_collision():
    global reset_required
    reset_required = True
    animate(hero, pos=HERO_START, on_finished=subtract_life)
```

This function is called when the animation is complete.

30 Egg collisions

You now need to add a function that will check if the hero has touched an egg or not. This function uses **colliderect()** to check this. If the hero touches an egg, the **egg_count** variable will be increased by the number of eggs in that lair. If the egg count reaches the target, the **game_complete** variable will be set to True and the player will win the game.

```python
def check_for_egg_collision(lair):
    global eggs_collected, game_complete
    if hero.colliderect(lair["eggs"]):
        lair["egg_hidden"] = True
        eggs_collected += lair["egg_count"]
        if eggs_collected >= EGG_TARGET:
            game_complete = True
```

This adds the number of eggs for the current lair to the player's egg count.

This checks if the number of eggs collected is greater than or equal to the **EGG_TARGET**.

31 Lose a life

Lastly, you need to define the **subtract_life()** function. Every time the player loses a life, this function will update the number of lives remaining. If there are no more lives left, the **game_over** variable will be set to True and the game will end.

```python
        game_complete = True


def subtract_life():
    global lives, reset_required, game_over
    lives -= 1
    if lives == 0:
        game_over = True
    reset_required = False
```

This variable is set to False, as the hero is already at the starting position.

32 Time to play

You are now ready for the quest. Try to collect all 20 eggs to win the game, but watch out for those dragons!

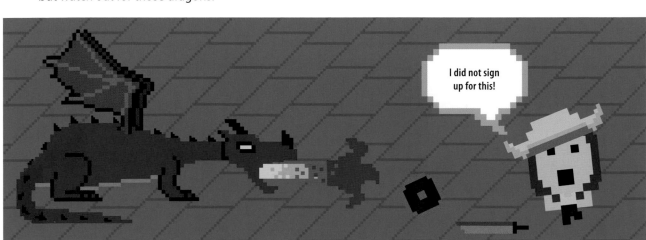

Hacks and tweaks

Add some more challenges to the quest and make the game even more engaging. Here are a few ideas to get you started.

I could use some help!

```
    if keyboard.d:
        hero2.x += MOVE_DISTANCE
        if hero2.x > WIDTH:
            hero2.x = WIDTH
    elif keyboard.a:
        hero2.x -= MOVE_DISTANCE
        if hero2.x < 0:
            hero2.x = 0
    elif keyboard.s:
        hero2.y += MOVE_DISTANCE
        if hero2.y > HEIGHT:
            hero2.y = HEIGHT
    elif keyboard.w:
        hero2.y -= MOVE_DISTANCE
        if hero2.y < 0:
            hero2.y = 0
```

◁ **Add another hero**

All this egg collecting can be a lot of work for one hero. You can add another hero to lend a hand. You'll need to add some new code and change some existing code to do this. Begin by changing the starting position of the current hero and adding a different one for the new hero. Then add some code to the **draw()** function to draw the second hero on the screen. Now add the code shown here to the **update()** function, which will make the second hero move on the screen using a new set of keys— W, A, S, D. Lastly, remember to add a parameter to all the functions that check for collisions so they check the collisions for both heroes.

This moves the second hero down.

▷ **Less predictable dragons**

Right now it's fairly easy to predict when a dragon will wake up. You can add an element of chance to each dragon's sleep cycle to make the game more challenging. For this, you'll first need to import the Random module at the top of your program. Then you'll need to add some code to the **update_sleeping_dragon()** function. This will randomly decide whether to wake up the dragon each time the function is called. To do this, add the line of code shown in black here to Step 23.

I know when the dragons will wake up next.

They are not as predictable as you think.

```
    if lair["sleep_counter"] >= lair["sleep_length"]:
        if random.choice([True, False]):
            lair["dragon"].image = "dragon-awake"
```

12

Reference

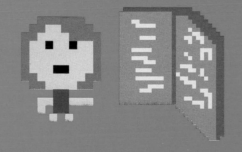

Project reference

This section contains the complete Python code for every game in this book, except for the hacks and tweaks. If your games don't run properly, check their scripts carefully against the code shown here.

Shoot the Fruit (page 48)

```python
from random import randint
apple = Actor("apple")

def draw():
    screen.clear()
    apple.draw()

def place_apple():
    apple.x = randint(10, 800)
    apple.y = randint(10, 600)

def on_mouse_down(pos):
    if apple.collidepoint(pos):
        print("Good shot!")
        place_apple()
    else:
        print("You missed!")
        quit()

place_apple()
```

Coin Collector (page 58)

```python
from random import randint

WIDTH = 400
HEIGHT = 400
score = 0
game_over = False

fox = Actor("fox")
fox.pos = 100, 100

coin = Actor("coin")
coin.pos = 200, 200
```

```
def draw():
    screen.fill("green")
    fox.draw()
    coin.draw()
    screen.draw.text("Score: " + str(score), color="black", topleft=(10, 10))

    if game_over:
        screen.fill("pink")
        screen.draw.text("Final Score: " + str(score), topleft=(10, 10), fontsize=60)

def place_coin():
    coin.x = randint(20, (WIDTH - 20))
    coin.y = randint(20, (HEIGHT - 20))

def time_up():
    global game_over
    game_over = True

def update():
    global score

    if keyboard.left:
        fox.x = fox.x - 2
    elif keyboard.right:
        fox.x = fox.x + 2
    elif keyboard.up:
        fox.y = fox.y - 2
    elif keyboard.down:
        fox.y = fox.y + 2

    coin_collected = fox.colliderect(coin)

    if coin_collected:
        score = score + 10
        place_coin()

clock.schedule(time_up, 7.0)
place_coin()
```

Follow the Numbers (page 68)

```
from random import randint

WIDTH = 400
HEIGHT = 400
```

```
dots = []
lines = []

next_dot = 0

for dot in range(0, 10):
    actor = Actor("dot")
    actor.pos = randint(20, WIDTH - 20), \
    randint(20, HEIGHT - 20)
    dots.append(actor)

def draw():
    screen.fill("black")
    number = 1
    for dot in dots:
        screen.draw.text(str(number), \
                         (dot.pos[0], dot.pos[1] + 12))
        dot.draw()
        number = number + 1
    for line in lines:
        screen.draw.line(line[0], line[1], (100, 0, 0))

def on_mouse_down(pos):
    global next_dot
    global lines
    if dots[next_dot].collidepoint(pos):
        if next_dot:
            lines.append((dots[next_dot - 1].pos, dots[next_dot].pos))
        next_dot = next_dot + 1
    else:
        lines = []
        next_dot = 0
```

Red Alert (page 80)

```
import random

FONT_COLOR = (255, 255, 255)
WIDTH = 800
HEIGHT = 600
CENTER_X = WIDTH / 2
CENTER_Y = HEIGHT / 2
CENTER = (CENTER_X, CENTER_Y)
FINAL_LEVEL = 6
START_SPEED = 10
COLORS = ["green", "blue"]
```

```
game_over = False
game_complete = False
current_level = 1
stars = []
animations = []

def draw():
    global stars, current_level, game_over, game_complete
    screen.clear()
    screen.blit("space", (0, 0))
    if game_over:
        display_message("GAME OVER!", "Try again.")
    elif game_complete:
        display_message("YOU WON!", "Well done.")
    else:
        for star in stars:
            star.draw()

def update():
    global stars
    if len(stars) == 0:
        stars = make_stars(current_level)

def make_stars(number_of_extra_stars):
    colors_to_create = get_colors_to_create(number_of_extra_stars)
    new_stars = create_stars(colors_to_create)
    layout_stars(new_stars)
    animate_stars(new_stars)
    return new_stars

def get_colors_to_create(number_of_extra_stars):
    colors_to_create = ["red"]
    for i in range(0, number_of_extra_stars):
        random_color = random.choice(COLORS)
        colors_to_create.append(random_color)
    return colors_to_create

def create_stars(colors_to_create):
    new_stars = []
    for color in colors_to_create:
        star = Actor(color + "-star")
        new_stars.append(star)
    return new_stars

def layout_stars(stars_to_layout):
    number_of_gaps = len(stars_to_layout) + 1
    gap_size = WIDTH / number_of_gaps
```

```python
    random.shuffle(stars_to_layout)
    for index, star in enumerate(stars_to_layout):
        new_x_pos = (index + 1) * gap_size
        star.x = new_x_pos

def animate_stars(stars_to_animate):
    for star in stars_to_animate:
        duration = START_SPEED - current_level
        star.anchor = ("center", "bottom")
        animation = animate(star, duration=duration, on_finished=handle_game_over, y=HEIGHT)
        animations.append(animation)

def handle_game_over():
    global game_over
    game_over = True

def on_mouse_down(pos):
    global stars, current_level
    for star in stars:
        if star.collidepoint(pos):
            if "red" in star.image:
                red_star_click()
            else:
                handle_game_over()

def red_star_click():
    global current_level, stars, animations, game_complete
    stop_animations(animations)
    if current_level == FINAL_LEVEL:
        game_complete = True
    else:
        current_level = current_level + 1
        stars = []
        animations = []

def stop_animations(animations_to_stop):
    for animation in animations_to_stop:
        if animation.running:
            animation.stop()

def display_message(heading_text, sub_heading_text):
    screen.draw.text(heading_text, fontsize=60, center=CENTER, color=FONT_COLOR)
    screen.draw.text(sub_heading_text,
                     fontsize=30,
                     center=(CENTER_X, CENTER_Y + 30),
                     color=FONT_COLOR)
```

Big Quiz (page 98)

```
WIDTH = 1280
HEIGHT = 720

main_box = Rect(0, 0, 820, 240)
timer_box = Rect(0, 0, 240, 240)
answer_box1 = Rect(0, 0, 495, 165)
answer_box2 = Rect(0, 0, 495, 165)
answer_box3 = Rect(0, 0, 495, 165)
answer_box4 = Rect(0, 0, 495, 165)

main_box.move_ip(50, 40)
timer_box.move_ip(990, 40)
answer_box1.move_ip(50, 358)
answer_box2.move_ip(735, 358)
answer_box3.move_ip(50, 538)
answer_box4.move_ip(735, 538)
answer_boxes = [answer_box1, answer_box2, answer_box3, answer_box4]

score = 0
time_left = 10

q1 = ["What is the capital of France?",
      "London", "Paris", "Berlin", "Tokyo", 2]

q2 = ["What is 5+7?",
      "12", "10", "14", "8", 1]

q3 = ["What is the seventh month of the year?",
      "April", "May", "June", "July", 4]

q4 = ["Which planet is closest to the Sun?",
      "Saturn", "Neptune", "Mercury", "Venus", 3]

q5 = ["Where are the pyramids?",
      "India", "Egypt", "Morocco", "Canada", 2]

questions = [q1, q2, q3, q4, q5]
question = questions.pop(0)

def draw():
    screen.fill("dim grey")
    screen.draw.filled_rect(main_box, "sky blue")
    screen.draw.filled_rect(timer_box, "sky blue")

    for box in answer_boxes:
        screen.draw.filled_rect(box, "orange")
```

```
        screen.draw.textbox(str(time_left), timer_box, color=("black"))
        screen.draw.textbox(question[0], main_box, color=("black"))

    index = 1
    for box in answer_boxes:
        screen.draw.textbox(question[index], box, color=("black"))
        index = index + 1

def game_over():
    global question, time_left
    message = "Game over. You got %s questions correct" % str(score)
    question = [message, "-", "-", "-", "-", 5]
    time_left = 0

def correct_answer():
    global question, score, time_left

    score = score + 1
    if questions:
        question = questions.pop(0)
        time_left = 10
    else:
        print("End of questions")
        game_over()

def on_mouse_down(pos):
    index = 1
    for box in answer_boxes:
        if box.collidepoint(pos):
            print("Clicked on answer " + str(index))
            if index == question[5]:
                print("You got it correct!")
                correct_answer()
            else:
                game_over()
        index = index + 1

def update_time_left():
    global time_left

    if time_left:
        time_left = time_left - 1
    else:
        game_over()

clock.schedule_interval(update_time_left, 1.0)
```

Balloon Flight (page 116)

```python
from random import randint

WIDTH = 800
HEIGHT = 600

balloon = Actor("balloon")
balloon.pos = 400, 300

bird = Actor("bird-up")
bird.pos = randint(800, 1600), randint(10, 200)

house = Actor("house")
house.pos = randint(800, 1600), 460

tree = Actor("tree")
tree.pos = randint(800, 1600), 450

bird_up = True
up = False
game_over = False
score = 0
number_of_updates = 0

scores = []

def update_high_scores():
    global score, scores
    filename = r"/Users/bharti/Desktop/python-games/balloon-flight/high-scores.txt"
    scores = []
    with open(filename, "r") as file:
        line = file.readline()
        high_scores = line.split()
        for high_score in high_scores:
            if(score > int(high_score)):
                scores.append(str(score) + " ")
                score = int(high_score)
            else:
                scores.append(str(high_score) + " ")
    with open(filename, "w") as file:
        for high_score in scores:
            file.write(high_score)

def display_high_scores():
    screen.draw.text("HIGH SCORES", (350, 150), color="black")
    y = 175
    position = 1
```

Remember, you'll need to change this gray bit of code to the high-scores.txt file's location on your own computer.

```
    for high_score in scores:
        screen.draw.text(str(position) + ". " + high_score, (350, y), color="black")
        y += 25
        position += 1

def draw():
    screen.blit("background", (0, 0))
    if not game_over:
        balloon.draw()
        bird.draw()
        house.draw()
        tree.draw()
        screen.draw.text("Score: " + str(score), (700, 5), color="black")
    else:
        display_high_scores()

def on_mouse_down():
    global up
    up = True
    balloon.y -= 50

def on_mouse_up():
    global up
    up = False

def flap():
    global bird_up
    if bird_up:
        bird.image = "bird-down"
        bird_up = False
    else:
        bird.image = "bird-up"
        bird_up = True

def update():
    global game_over, score, number_of_updates
    if not game_over:
        if not up:
            balloon.y += 1

        if bird.x > 0:
            bird.x -= 4
            if number_of_updates == 9:
                flap()
                number_of_updates = 0
            else:
                number_of_updates += 1
```

```
        else:
            bird.x = randint(800, 1600)
            bird.y = randint(10, 200)
            score += 1
            number_of_updates = 0

        if house.right > 0:
            house.x -= 2
        else:
            house.x = randint(800, 1600)
            score += 1

        if tree.right > 0:
            tree.x -= 2
        else:
            tree.x = randint(800, 1600)
            score += 1

        if balloon.top < 0 or balloon.bottom > 560:
            game_over = True
            update_high_scores()

        if balloon.collidepoint(bird.x, bird.y) or \
            balloon.collidepoint(house.x, house.y) or \
            balloon.collidepoint(tree.x, tree.y):
                game_over = True
                update_high_scores()
```

Dance Challenge (page 136)

```
from random import randint

WIDTH = 800
HEIGHT = 600
CENTER_X = WIDTH / 2
CENTER_Y = HEIGHT / 2

move_list = []
display_list = []

score = 0
current_move = 0
count = 4
dance_length = 4

say_dance = False
show_countdown = True
```

```
moves_complete = False
game_over = False


dancer = Actor("dancer-start")
dancer.pos = CENTER_X + 5, CENTER_Y - 40


up = Actor("up")
up.pos = CENTER_X, CENTER_Y + 110
right = Actor("right")
right.pos = CENTER_X + 60, CENTER_Y + 170
down = Actor("down")
down.pos = CENTER_X, CENTER_Y + 230
left = Actor("left")
left.pos = CENTER_X - 60, CENTER_Y + 170


def draw():
    global game_over, score, say_dance
    global count, show_countdown
    if not game_over:
        screen.clear()
        screen.blit("stage", (0, 0))
        dancer.draw()
        up.draw()
        down.draw()
        right.draw()
        left.draw()
        screen.draw.text("Score: " +
                        str(score), color="black",
                        topleft=(10, 10))
        if say_dance:
            screen.draw.text("Dance!", color="black",
                            topleft=(CENTER_X - 65, 150), fontsize=60)
        if show_countdown:
            screen.draw.text(str(count), color="black",
                            topleft=(CENTER_X - 8, 150), fontsize=60)
    else:
        screen.clear()
        screen.blit("stage", (0, 0))
        screen.draw.text("Score: " +
                        str(score), color="black",
                        topleft=(10, 10))
        screen.draw.text("GAME OVER!", color="black",
                        topleft=(CENTER_X - 130, 220), fontsize=60)
    return

def reset_dancer():
    global game_over
```

```
    if not game_over:
        dancer.image = "dancer-start"
        up.image = "up"
        right.image = "right"
        down.image = "down"
        left.image = "left"
    return

def update_dancer(move):
    global game_over
    if not game_over:
        if move == 0:
            up.image = "up-lit"
            dancer.image = "dancer-up"
            clock.schedule(reset_dancer, 0.5)
        elif move == 1:
            right.image = "right-lit"
            dancer.image = "dancer-right"
            clock.schedule(reset_dancer, 0.5)
        elif move == 2:
            down.image = "down-lit"
            dancer.image = "dancer-down"
            clock.schedule(reset_dancer, 0.5)
        else:
            left.image = "left-lit"
            dancer.image = "dancer-left"
            clock.schedule(reset_dancer, 0.5)
    return

def display_moves():
    global move_list, display_list, dance_length
    global say_dance, show_countdown, current_move
    if display_list:
        this_move = display_list[0]
        display_list = display_list[1:]
        if this_move == 0:
            update_dancer(0)
            clock.schedule(display_moves, 1)
        elif this_move == 1:
            update_dancer(1)
            clock.schedule(display_moves, 1)
        elif this_move == 2:
            update_dancer(2)
            clock.schedule(display_moves, 1)
        else:
            update_dancer(3)
            clock.schedule(display_moves, 1)
```

```python
    else:
        say_dance = True
        show_countdown = False
    return

def countdown():
    global count, game_over, show_countdown
    if count > 1:
        count = count - 1
        clock.schedule(countdown, 1)
    else:
        show_countdown = False
        display_moves()
    return

def generate_moves():
    global move_list, dance_length, count
    global show_countdown, say_dance
    count = 4
    move_list = []
    say_dance = False
    for move in range(0, dance_length):
        rand_move = randint(0, 3)
        move_list.append(rand_move)
        display_list.append(rand_move)
    show_countdown = True
    countdown()
    return

def next_move():
    global dance_length, current_move, moves_complete
    if current_move < dance_length - 1:
        current_move = current_move + 1
    else:
        moves_complete = True
    return

def on_key_up(key):
    global score, game_over, move_list, current_move
    if key == keys.UP:
        update_dancer(0)
        if move_list[current_move] == 0:
            score = score + 1
            next_move()
        else:
            game_over = True
    elif key == keys.RIGHT:
```

```
        update_dancer(1)
        if move_list[current_move] == 1:
            score = score + 1
            next_move()
        else:
            game_over = True
    elif key == keys.DOWN:
        update_dancer(2)
        if move_list[current_move] == 2:
            score = score + 1
            next_move()
        else:
            game_over = True
    elif key == keys.LEFT:
        update_dancer(3)
        if move_list[current_move] == 3:
            score = score + 1
            next_move()
        else:
            game_over = True
    return

generate_moves()
music.play("vanishing-horizon")

def update():
    global game_over, current_move, moves_complete
    if not game_over:
        if moves_complete:
            generate_moves()
            moves_complete = False
            current_move = 0
    else:
        music.stop()
```

Happy Garden (page 154)

```
from random import randint
import time

WIDTH = 800
HEIGHT = 600
CENTER_X = WIDTH / 2
CENTER_Y = HEIGHT / 2

game_over = False
finalised = False
```

```python
garden_happy = True
fangflower_collision = False

time_elapsed = 0
start_time = time.time()

cow = Actor("cow")
cow.pos = 100, 500

flower_list = []
wilted_list = []
fangflower_list = []
fangflower_vy_list = []
fangflower_vx_list = []

def draw():
    global game_over, time_elapsed, finalized
    if not game_over:
        screen.clear()
        screen.blit("garden", (0, 0))
        cow.draw()
        for flower in flower_list:
            flower.draw()
        for fangflower in fangflower_list:
            fangflower.draw()
        time_elapsed = int(time.time() - start_time)
        screen.draw.text(
            "Garden happy for: " +
            str(time_elapsed) + " seconds",
            topleft=(10, 10), color="black"
        )
    else:
        if not finalized:
            cow.draw()
            screen.draw.text(
                "Garden happy for: " +
                str(time_elapsed) + " seconds",
                topleft=(10, 10), color="black"
            )
            if (not garden_happy):
                screen.draw.text(
                    "GARDEN UNHAPPY - GAME OVER!", color="black",
                    topleft=(10, 50)
                )
                finalized = True
            else:
                screen.draw.text(
```

```
                    "FANGFLOWER ATTACK - GAME OVER!", color="black",
                    topleft=(10, 50)
            )
                finalized = True
    return

def new_flower():
    global flower_list, wilted_list
    flower_new = Actor("flower")
    flower_new.pos = randint(50, WIDTH - 50), randint(150, HEIGHT - 100)
    flower_list.append(flower_new)
    wilted_list.append("happy")
    return

def add_flowers():
    global game_over
    if not game_over:
        new_flower()
        clock.schedule(add_flowers, 4)
    return

def check_wilt_times():
    global wilted_list, game_over, garden_happy
    if wilted_list:
        for wilted_since in wilted_list:
            if (not wilted_since == "happy"):
                time_wilted = int(time.time() - wilted_since)
                if (time_wilted) > 10.0:
                    garden_happy = False
                    game_over = True
                    break
    return

def wilt_flower():
    global flower_list, wilted_list, game_over
    if not game_over:
        if flower_list:
            rand_flower = randint(0, len(flower_list) - 1)
            if (flower_list[rand_flower].image == "flower"):
                flower_list[rand_flower].image = "flower-wilt"
                wilted_list[rand_flower] = time.time()
        clock.schedule(wilt_flower, 3)
    return

def check_flower_collision():
    global cow, flower_list, wilted_list
    index = 0
```

```
    for flower in flower_list:
        if (flower.colliderect(cow) and
                flower.image == "flower-wilt"):
            flower.image = "flower"
            wilted_list[index] = "happy"
            break
        index = index + 1
    return


def check_fangflower_collision():
    global cow, fangflower_list, fangflower_collision
    global game_over
    for fangflower in fangflower_list:
        if fangflower.colliderect(cow):
            cow.image = "zap"
            game_over = True
            break
    return


def velocity():
    random_dir = randint(0, 1)
    random_velocity = randint(2, 3)
    if random_dir == 0:
        return -random_velocity
    else:
        return random_velocity


def mutate():
    global flower_list, fangflower_list, fangflower_vy_list
    global fangflower_vx_list, game_over
    if not game_over and flower_list:
        rand_flower = randint(0, len(flower_list) - 1)
        fangflower_pos_x = flower_list[rand_flower].x
        fangflower_pos_y = flower_list[rand_flower].y
        del flower_list[rand_flower]
        fangflower = Actor("fangflower")
        fangflower.pos = fangflower_pos_x, fangflower_pos_y
        fangflower_vx = velocity()
        fangflower_vy = velocity()
        fangflower = fangflower_list.append(fangflower)
        fangflower_vx_list.append(fangflower_vx)
        fangflower_vy_list.append(fangflower_vy)
        clock.schedule(mutate, 20)
    return


def update_fangflowers():
    global fangflower_list, game_over
```

```
    if not game_over:
        index = 0
        for fangflower in fangflower_list:
            fangflower_vx = fangflower_vx_list[index]
            fangflower_vy = fangflower_vy_list[index]
            fangflower.x = fangflower.x + fangflower_vx
            fangflower.y = fangflower.y + fangflower_vy
            if fangflower.left < 0:
                fangflower_vx_list[index] = -fangflower_vx
            if fangflower.right > WIDTH:
                fangflower_vx_list[index] = -fangflower_vx
            if fangflower.top < 150:
                fangflower_vy_list[index] = -fangflower_vy
            if fangflower.bottom > HEIGHT:
                fangflower_vy_list[index] = -fangflower_vy
            index = index + 1
    return

def reset_cow():
    global game_over
    if not game_over:
        cow.image = "cow"
    return

add_flowers()
wilt_flower()

def update():
    global score, game_over, fangflower_collision
    global flower_list, fangflower_list, time_elapsed
    fangflower_collision = check_fangflower_collision()
    check_wilt_times()
    if not game_over:
        if keyboard.space:
            cow.image = "cow-water"
            clock.schedule(reset_cow, 0.5)
            check_flower_collision()
        if keyboard.left and cow.x > 0:
            cow.x -= 5
        elif keyboard.right and cow.x < WIDTH:
            cow.x += 5
        elif keyboard.up and cow.y > 150:
            cow.y -= 5
        elif keyboard.down and cow.y < HEIGHT:
            cow.y += 5
        if time_elapsed > 15 and not fangflower_list:
            mutate()
        update_fangflowers()
```

Sleeping Dragons (page 176)

```python
import math


WIDTH = 800
HEIGHT = 600
CENTER_X = WIDTH / 2
CENTER_Y = HEIGHT / 2
CENTER = (CENTER_X, CENTER_Y)
FONT_COLOR = (0, 0, 0)
EGG_TARGET = 20
HERO_START = (200, 300)
ATTACK_DISTANCE = 200
DRAGON_WAKE_TIME = 2
EGG_HIDE_TIME = 2
MOVE_DISTANCE = 5


lives = 3
eggs_collected = 0
game_over = False
game_complete = False
reset_required = False


easy_lair = {
    "dragon": Actor("dragon-asleep", pos=(600, 100)),
    "eggs": Actor("one-egg", pos=(400, 100)),
    "egg_count": 1,
    "egg_hidden": False,
    "egg_hide_counter": 0,
    "sleep_length": 10,
    "sleep_counter": 0,
    "wake_counter": 0
}


medium_lair = {
    "dragon": Actor("dragon-asleep", pos=(600, 300)),
    "eggs": Actor("two-eggs", pos=(400, 300)),
    "egg_count": 2,
    "egg_hidden": False,
    "egg_hide_counter": 0,
    "sleep_length": 7,
    "sleep_counter": 0,
    "wake_counter": 0
}


hard_lair = {
    "dragon": Actor("dragon-asleep", pos=(600, 500)),
    "eggs": Actor("three-eggs", pos=(400, 500)),
```

```
        "egg_count": 3,
        "egg_hidden": False,
        "egg_hide_counter": 0,
        "sleep_length": 4,
        "sleep_counter": 0,
        "wake_counter": 0
}

lairs = [easy_lair, medium_lair, hard_lair]
hero = Actor("hero", pos=HERO_START)

def draw():
    global lairs, eggs_collected, lives, game_complete
    screen.clear()
    screen.blit("dungeon", (0, 0))
    if game_over:
        screen.draw.text("GAME OVER!", fontsize=60, center=CENTER, color=FONT_COLOR)
    elif game_complete:
        screen.draw.text("YOU WON!", fontsize=60, center=CENTER, color=FONT_COLOR)
    else:
        hero.draw()
        draw_lairs(lairs)
        draw_counters(eggs_collected, lives)

def draw_lairs(lairs_to_draw):
    for lair in lairs_to_draw:
        lair["dragon"].draw()
        if lair["egg hidden"] is False:
            lair["eggs"].draw()

def draw_counters(eggs_collected, lives):
    screen.blit("egg-count", (0, HEIGHT - 30))
    screen.draw.text(str(eggs_collected),
                     fontsize=40,
                     pos=(30, HEIGHT - 30),
                     color=FONT_COLOR)
    screen.blit("life-count", (60, HEIGHT - 30))
    screen.draw.text(str(lives),
                     fontsize=40,
                     pos=(90, HEIGHT - 30),
                     color=FONT_COLOR)
    screen.draw.text(str(lives),
                     fontsize=40,
                     pos=(90, HEIGHT - 30),
                     color=FONT_COLOR)
```

```
def update():
    if keyboard.right:
        hero.x += MOVE_DISTANCE
        if hero.x > WIDTH:
            hero.x = WIDTH
    elif keyboard.left:
        hero.x -= MOVE_DISTANCE
        if hero.x < 0:
            hero.x = 0
    elif keyboard.down:
        hero.y += MOVE_DISTANCE
        if hero.y > HEIGHT:
            hero.y = HEIGHT
    elif keyboard.up:
        hero.y -= MOVE_DISTANCE
        if hero.y < 0:
            hero.y = 0
    check_for_collisions()

def update_lairs():
    global lairs, hero, lives
    for lair in lairs:
        if lair["dragon"].image == "dragon-asleep":
            update_sleeping_dragon(lair)
        elif lair["dragon"].image == "dragon-awake":
            update_waking_dragon(lair)
        update_egg(lair)

clock.schedule_interval(update_lairs, 1)

def update_sleeping_dragon(lair):
    if lair["sleep_counter"] >= lair["sleep_length"]:
        lair["dragon"].image = "dragon-awake"
        lair["sleep_counter"] = 0
    else:
        lair["sleep_counter"] += 1

def update_waking_dragon(lair):
    if lair["wake_counter"] >= DRAGON_WAKE_TIME:
        lair["dragon"].image = "dragon-asleep"
        lair["wake_counter"] = 0
    else:
        lair["wake_counter"] += 1

def update_egg(lair):
    if lair["egg_hidden"] is True:
        if lair["egg_hide_counter"] >= EGG_HIDE_TIME:
```

```
            lair["egg_hidden"] = False
            lair["egg_hide_counter"] = 0
        else:
            lair["egg_hide_counter"] += 1

def check_for_collisions():
    global lairs, eggs_collected, lives, reset_required, game_complete
    for lair in lairs:
        if lair["egg_hidden"] is False:
            check_for_egg_collision(lair)
        if lair["dragon"].image == "dragon-awake" and reset_required is False:
            check_for_dragon_collision(lair)

def check_for_dragon_collision(lair):
    x_distance = hero.x - lair["dragon"].x
    y_distance = hero.y - lair["dragon"].y
    distance = math.hypot(x_distance, y_distance)
    if distance < ATTACK_DISTANCE:
        handle_dragon_collision()

def handle_dragon_collision():
    global reset_required
    reset_required = True
    animate(hero, pos=HERO_START, on_finished=subtract_life)

def check_for_egg_collision(lair):
    global eggs_collected, game_complete
    if hero.colliderect(lair["eggs"]):
        lair["egg_hidden"] = True
        eggs_collected += lair["egg_count"]
        if eggs_collected >= EGG_TARGET:
            game_complete = True

def subtract_life():
    global lives, reset_required, game_over
    lives -= 1
    if lives == 0:
        game_over = True
    reset_required = False
```

You've got really bad breath, dude!

Glossary

animation
A process in which images are displayed one after another to make it look like something's moving.

Boolean expression
A statement that is either True or False, leading to two possible outcomes.

branch
A point in a program where different options are available to choose from.

bug
An error in a program's code that makes it behave in an unexpected way.

call
To use a function in a program.

command line
The screen that lets you enter commands into the Command Prompt or Terminal window.

Command Prompt
An application on Windows computers that allows a user to enter and execute commands.

comment
A text note added to a program that makes the code easier to understand and is ignored by the program when it runs.

condition
A "True or False" statement used to make a decision in a program. See also *Boolean expression*.

constant
A variable whose value should stay the same throughout a program. Programmers use capital letters when naming constants to let other programmers know that their values should not be changed. See also *variable*.

coordinates
A pair of numbers that pinpoint an exact location. Usually written as (x, y).

data
Information, such as text, symbols, and numerical values.

dictionary
A collection of data items stored in pairs, such as countries and their capital cities.

debug
To look for and correct errors in a program.

encryption
A way of encoding data so that only certain people can read or access it.

event
Something a computer program can react to, such as a key being pressed or the mouse being clicked.

file
A collection of data stored with a name.

flag variable
A variable that can have two states, such as True and False.

float
A number with a decimal point in it.

flowchart
A diagram that shows a program as a sequence of steps and decisions.

function
Code that carries out a specific task. Also called a procedure, subprogram, or subroutine.

global variable
A variable that can be used throughout every part of a program. See also *local variable*.

graphics
Visual elements on a screen, such as text, pictures, icons, and symbols.

GUI
The GUI, or graphical user interface, is the name for the buttons and windows that make up the part of the program you can see and interact with.

hack
An ingenious change to code that makes it do something new or simplifies it. (Also, accessing a computer without permission.)

hacker
A person who breaks into a computer system. "White hat" hackers work for computer security companies and look for problems in order to fix them. "Black hat" hackers break into computer systems to cause harm or to make profit from them.

indent
When a block of code is placed farther to the right than the previous block. An indent is usually four spaces. Every line in a particular block of code must be indented by the same amount.

index number
A number given to an item in a list. In Python, the index number of the first item will be 0, the second item 1, and so on.

input
Data that is entered into a computer. Keyboards, mice, and microphones can be used to input data.

integer
A whole number. An integer does not contain a decimal point and is not written as a fraction.

interface
The means by which the user interacts with software or hardware. See *GUI*.

keyword
A word that has a special meaning in a program. All programming languages have a set of keywords. These words cannot be used to name variables or functions.

library
A collection of functions that can be reused in other projects.

list
A collection of items stored in numbered order.

local variable
A variable that works only within a limited part of a program, such as a function. See also *global variable*.

loop
A part of a program that repeats itself, so you don't need to type out the same piece of code multiple times.

module
A package of ready-made code that can be imported into a Python program, making lots of useful functions available.

nested loop
A loop inside another loop.

operating system (OS)
The program that controls everything on a computer. Windows, macOS, and Linux are operating systems.

operator
A symbol that performs a specific function: for example, "+" (addition) or "−" (subtraction).

output
Data that is produced by a computer program and viewed by the user.

parameter
A value given to a function. The value of a parameter is assigned by the line of code that calls the function.

pixels
Tiny dots that make up a digital image.

program
A set of instructions that a computer follows in order to complete a task.

programming language
A language that is used to give instructions to a computer.

Python
A popular programming language created by Guido van Rossum. It is a great language for beginners to learn.

random
A function in a computer program that allows unpredictable outcomes. Useful when creating games.

recursion
Creating a loop by telling a function to call itself.

return value
The variable or data that is passed back after a function has been called (run).

run
The command to make a program start.

software
Programs that run on a computer and control how it works.

statement
The smallest complete instruction a programming language can be broken down into.

string
A series of characters. Strings can contain numbers, letters, or symbols, such as a colon.

syntax
The rules that determine how code must be written in order for it to work properly.

Terminal
An application on Mac computers that allows a user to enter and execute commands.

toggle
To switch between two different settings.

Unicode
A universal code used by computers to represent thousands of symbols and text characters.

variable
A place to store data that can change in a program, such as the player's score. A variable has a name and a value. See also *global variable* and *local variable*.

Index

Acknowledgments

DK Publishing would like to thank Caroline Hunt for proofreading; Jonathan Burd for the index; Daniel Pope for creating Pygame Zero; Jason Shaw at audionautix.com for the music for Dance Challenge; Chloe Parry, Phoebe Parry, and Joshua Parry for user testing; Aashirwad Jain for code testing; and Isha Sharma for editorial assistance.